FEARLESS CONVERSATION™

WHY IS JESUS SO RADICAL?

DISCUSSIONS FROM MATTHEW AND LUKE

LEADER GUIDE

Loveland, CO

Group resources really work!
This Group resource incorporates our R.E.A.L. approach to ministry. It reinforces a growing friendship with Jesus, encourages long-term learning, and results in life transformation, because it's:

Relational—Learner-to-learner interaction enhances learning and builds Christian friendships.

Experiential—What learners experience through discussion and action sticks with them up to 9 times longer than what they simply hear or read.

Applicable—The aim of Christian education is to equip learners to be both hearers and doers of God's Word.

Learner-based—Learners understand and retain more when the learning process takes into consideration how they learn best.

Fearless Conversation: Why Is Jesus So Radical?
Discussions from Matthew and Luke
Leader Guide

Copyright © 2014 Group Publishing, Inc.

All rights reserved. No part of this book may be reproduced in any manner whatsoever without prior written permission from the publisher, except where noted in the text and in the case of brief quotations embodied in critical articles and reviews. For information, go to group.com/permissions.

Visit our website: **group.com**

Fearless Conversation adult Sunday school curriculum is created by the amazing adult ministry team at Group. Contributing writers for this quarter are:

Susan Lawrence
Larry Shallenberger
Doug Schmidt
Thomas Smith

Unless otherwise indicated, all Scripture quotations are taken from the *Holy Bible*, New International Version® NIV® Copyright © 1973, 1978, 1984, 2011 by Biblica, Inc.® Used by permission. All rights reserved worldwide.

ISBN 978-1-4707-1349-2

Printed in the United States of America.

10 9 8 7 6 5 4 3 2 1   21 20 19 18 17 16 15 14

CONTENTS

Lesson 1: Why did God come as a baby? (Luke 2:1-20) — 9

Lesson 2: Can we really beat temptation? (Matthew 4:1-11) — 17

Lesson 3: What does it really mean to follow Jesus? (Matthew 4:18-25) — 25

Lesson 4: How can I tell if Jesus cares enough to act in my situation? (Matthew 9:18-26) — 33

Lesson 5: What does it mean if Jesus really is God's Son? (Luke 9:18-36) — 41

Lesson 6: Why did Jesus tell such confusing stories? (Matthew 13:24-45) — 51

Lesson 7: Was Jesus racist, or sexist—or both? (Matthew 15:21-28) — 61

Lesson 8: What's Jesus got against grown-ups? (Luke 18:15-17) — 69

Lesson 9: What was really going on at Jesus' "Triumphal Entry" into Jerusalem? (Luke 19:29-44) — 77

Lesson 10: What if God wants more than I want to give? (Matthew 26:36-55) — 87

Lesson 11: Did God really disown Jesus on the cross? (Matthew 27:32-55) — 95

Lesson 12: Resurrection seems so impossible…how can I believe in a literal "Easter" story? (Matthew 27:62–28:15) — 103

Lesson 13: How can I know Jesus is really alive today? (Luke 24:36-53) — 111

ARE YOU READY FOR
FEARLESS CONVERSATION?

Jesus loved getting people to think. He asked provocative question, such as "What do you want?" "Where is your faith?" and "Who do you say that I am?" And he often asked just one simple question: "What do you think?"

On the flip side of this, Jesus never quizzed his followers on facts such as "Where was I born?" or "How many commandments are there?" He didn't pass out fill-in-the-blank worksheets. And he didn't offer simple, pat answers. Instead he helped people wonder, grapple, and wrestle with the hard questions of life and faith. That's what Fearless Conversation is all about.

Through this Sunday school curriculum, you'll lead adults on a 13-week journey of respectful and faith-filled conversation. This involves:

- seeking to understand others and their perspectives

- listening before you speak

- asking questions that likely don't have an easy answer

- inviting others to talk instead of listen to you lecture

- having people form small groups, even if it means moving a few chairs

- avoiding judgment if someone expresses a different opinion

- trusting that God can guide the conversation—because he can!

HERE'S WHAT A LESSON LOOKS LIKE.

Each week you'll guide participants through four sections of the lesson. You'll need this book, and each person will need his or her own copy of the participant guide. These guides are not photocopiable, so be sure each person has their own book.

GREETING

You'll welcome everyone warmly and introduce the topic of conversation for the day. Participants will get into smaller groups during this time, which will help them share more openly and also allow time for everyone to participate in the conversation. If you try to keep everyone in one large group it will be difficult for people to truly engage, so be sure you guide people in keeping the groups to no more than four people per group.

GROUNDING

This is where you read the Scripture for the week. You'll find the Bible content for every lesson in this leader guide, and it is also always provided in the participant guide. Feel free to read the Scripture passages from the guide or from your own Bible. After hearing God's Word read aloud, each person will have the opportunity to follow the inductive method of writing down first responses, questions, thoughts, or ideas that are sparked by the reading.

GRAPPLING

Here's where the conversation deepens. You'll guide everyone through a few questions that are intentionally challenging to answer. These won't have easy answers, and you won't have a fill-in-the-blank option. Everyone will wrestle with the questions that the lesson provides, as well as their own questions that they're wondering about. You'll be guided to pray before each "Grappling" section, asking God to guide the conversation. And you'll also remind everyone to treat each other with respect.

GROWING

Here's where the personal application comes in. Participants will have the chance to reflect on what God's Word, as shared in this lesson, means to their own lives and determine what their personal response is.

Throughout each lesson you'll also find two other helps:

BEHIND THE SCENES

These sections of commentary are provided for you and they are also in the participant guide so everyone can have access to these readings. You can read them ahead of time, and encourage those in your class to read them either ahead of time or during the lesson. These notes from Bible scholars will help everyone have additional context into history, language, culture, and other relevant information.

LEADER LEARNINGS

These notes to you will help you improve your leadership skills. You'll find tips on group dynamics and on being a stellar leader of fearless conversations.

GUIDELINES FOR A SUCCESSFUL CLASS

Be a facilitator, not a lecturer. You're here to direct the conversation, help others get involved, and keep the discussion moving along. This curriculum is about everyone being a part of the conversation, which means it's more about the participants than it is about you.

Direct adults into small groups. When people are in groups of about four, they will open up more easily and share more openly. Asking a question in front of 30 people is intimidating, and no one wants to look like a fool! Smaller groups also allow everyone the opportunity to talk and express their thoughts. If the groups are too large, there simply won't be enough time for each person to contribute. There are sections of each lesson that involve the entire group, but when the lesson calls for small group discussion, be sure you help adults get into those groups.

Encourage relationships. People are more likely to keep coming back once they've made a few friends. Always share your name and invite others to do so as well. If topics of conversation during the lesson are especially compelling for your group, see if a few people want to keep talking about it over coffee later in the week. Plus, friends are more likely to pray for each other, support each other, and encourage each other.

Expect the unexpected. The conversations that will begin in your class could very easily get off track. That's okay! God is involved in this conversation too, and he might have a different plan. Be open to the different directions the Holy Spirit may lead. Take advantage of teachable moments. Don't panic! Instead, relax and trust God to be the guide.

Have a sense of divine anticipation. Approach each class with a heart full of anticipation over what God might do that day. God is alive and present with you and your class. Always prepare by praying, asking God to help you see his hand at work in the conversation. And if you start to have a moment of stress as the lesson takes a turn you didn't anticipate, it's okay to just stop everyone and say, "Let's refocus by taking a moment to ask God to guide us," and then pray for just that.

LEADER GUIDE

LESSON 1:
WHY DID GOD COME AS A BABY?

LEADER PREP

- Read the entire lesson ahead of time. Also read the corresponding pages in the Why Is Jesus So Radical? Participant Guide as there may be additional material provided there that will be helpful to you.

- You'll find "Behind the Scenes" boxes with Bible commentary provided throughout this lesson. They're there to help you gain a better understanding of the Bible. The people in your group will have these too.

- Pray. Lots.

FOR EXTRA IMPACT
Put a goldfish in a glass bowl somewhere in your meeting area. If you don't have or can't easily get a goldfish, that's okay—but it will be more fun if you can bring one along.

Prep Notes:

GREETING

BEHIND THE SCENES

Luke 2:1-20 describes Joseph and Mary's journey to Bethlehem and the birth of Jesus. Certainly it had been difficult for them to endure the stares and overhear the snickers of acquaintances who noticed that Mary had become pregnant prior to the completion of their marriage. Now she and Joseph were forced by the Romans to travel from their home in Nazareth to his ancestral home of Bethlehem. This was a journey of about 70 miles. Although popular renditions of this trip usually show Mary riding a donkey, she and Joseph probably weren't wealthy enough to own one. It's more likely that they had to walk all the way, even though Mary was close to her time to deliver.

The exact date of Jesus' birth is impossible to calculate. According to Luke 2:2, the census occurred when Quirinius was governor of Syria. His first term occurred from 6 to 4 B.C., so Jesus was likely born between those dates. Unfortunately, the date of Jesus' birth was miscalculated when the Christian calendar was created hundreds of years later.

- Welcome everyone and be sure to introduce yourself.

- Be sure everyone has a copy of the participant guide.

- Let everyone know you'll be moving through Lesson 1 today, so they can find that section in their guide to use throughout today's lesson.

Then ask:

Where were you born? Call it out to the group and let's see where everyone is from!

Let people call out the cities or states they were born in—you might help people find new connections to long-lost neighbors and friends. Then say:

LESSON 2: CAN WE REALLY BEAT TEMPTATION?

LEADER PREP

- Read the entire lesson ahead of time. Also read the corresponding pages in the Why Is Jesus So Radical? Participant Guide as there may be additional material provided there that will be helpful to you.

- You'll find "Behind the Scenes" boxes with Bible commentary provided throughout this lesson. They're there to help you gain a better understanding of the Bible. The people in your group will have these too.

- Spend time talking with God about what he wants to teach you and the people in this class through today's lesson.

FOR EXTRA IMPACT

Scatter simple objects on a table or tray where everyone can see, or place several items on each table. Suggested items: money, cellphone, chocolate, pencil, toy car, permanent marker, matches, candle, a small ball, and hand sanitizer. If you don't want to gather the items, that's okay—but seeing items will help spur imaginations.

LESSON 2: CAN WE REALLY BEAT TEMPTATION? **17**

GREETING

BEHIND THE SCENES

Satan in Hebrew means "adversary" or "accuser." Matthew 4:1-11 describes Jesus' interactions with Satan in the wilderness. These interactions can be compared to the first temptation in the Garden with Adam and Eve (Genesis 3:1-7) and the period of wandering in the wilderness with the nation of Israel. As with Eve, Satan directly approaches an isolated Jesus and challenges what God has said he can and should do. Like Israel's 40 years in the wilderness, Jesus' 40 days include temptation by hunger (Exodus 16:2-8), temptation to test God (Exodus 17:1-4), and temptation of idolatry (Exodus 32). Unlike the temptations with Adam and Eve and the Israelites, Jesus boldly responds with the words of God, quoting Deuteronomy 8:3, 6:16, and 6:13. Unlike Adam and Eve and the Israelites, Jesus doesn't give in to temptation.

Luke's account of the temptations (4:1-13) describes them as a process, a journey by which Satan and Jesus were together. Satan chose three specific times to tempt Jesus, and Jesus responded with truth each time. Satan's power is no match for God's truth.

- Welcome everyone and be sure to introduce yourself.

- Be sure everyone has a copy of the participant guide.

- Let everyone know you'll be moving through Lesson 2 today, so they can find that section in their participant guide and use it to prompt them through today's lesson.

- Explain that there are many "Behind the Scenes" commentary notes throughout the lesson. These can be read by participants as they come to that section of the lesson—or people who want to plan ahead can read them during the week to be ready for the next lesson.

Then ask:

Think about a time when you were younger and you did something you knew you weren't supposed to do. I'll pause and let you think about that "I-shouldn't-have-done-that"

moment. Pause for 15 seconds. **Okay, got something in mind? Let's get into small groups and talk about it.**

Have everyone get into groups of no more than four.

- **Share a word or phrase that describes what led up to your shouldn't-have-done-that moment. Why did you do something you knew you weren't supposed to do?**

Talk about it in your small group. The questions are also included in your participant guide. Be sure you introduce yourselves, too. You'll have 4 minutes.

Allow about 4 minutes for people to introduce themselves and discuss this question. Give them a 30 second "wrap-up" alert, and then continue.

Thanks for sharing in your groups and getting to know each other a little better. Today we're going to be grappling with questions related to stuff we shouldn't do. The Bible calls this *sin*. First, we need to figure out what we really mean by the word *sin*. So let's dig in.

Draw everyone's attention to the small items you brought. If you weren't able to place items where everyone will see them, refer them to the pictures in their participant guides.

These are everyday items. With your group, choose two or three of these items to talk about. Decide what those items may or may not have to do with sin. It's okay if you have different opinions! You'll have about 4 minutes.

- **What do these items have to do with sin?**

After 4 minutes, invite groups to share a few observations with the larger group. Then continue.

These items we had to choose from were pretty neutral—they are normally helpful in our lives, but they could also be used for activities that are not healthy. Today we're digging into Satan tempting Jesus in the wilderness. Before we do, consider how using these everyday objects in very different ways is related to temptation.

- **Where in your daily life do you tend to encounter temptation to do something you know you shouldn't do?**

As the leader, briefly share your response to this question first. Then allow time for several other people to respond to this question to the whole group. Then continue.

! LEADER LEARNING

Keep groups small. (If you're in a smaller church, your group may be small already—and that's great!) Avoid letting larger groups gather, even if the room arrangement makes it more convenient or people prefer to stay with all their friends. Groups of four give everyone the time, safety, and opportunity they need in order to share.

GROUNDING

Let's get grounded in God's Word so we can understand more about how Satan and Jesus interacted and what that means for our everyday living. Today's Bible account is from Matthew 4:1-11. At the time of this interaction between Satan and Jesus, Jesus had just begun his ministry. John the Baptist had baptized him, yet Jesus hadn't preached or taught, performed any miracles, called his disciples, or stirred up trouble among the leaders of his day.

Let's read Matthew's account.

Read Matthew 4:1-11 aloud, or ask for a volunteer from your group to read it aloud. Encourage everyone else to follow along in their own Bibles or in their participant guides.

God's Word: Matthew 4:1-11

¹ Then Jesus was led by the Spirit into the wilderness to be tempted by the devil. ² After fasting forty days and forty nights, he was hungry. ³ The tempter came to him and said, "If you are the Son of God, tell these stones to become bread."

⁴ Jesus answered, "It is written: 'Man shall not live on bread alone, but on every word that comes from the mouth of God.'"

⁵ Then the devil took him to the holy city and had him stand on the highest point of the temple. ⁶ "If you are the Son of God," he said, "throw yourself down. For it is written: 'He will command his angels concerning you, and they will lift you up in their hands, so that you will not strike your foot against a stone.'"

⁷ Jesus answered him, "It is also written: 'Do not put the Lord your God to the test.'"

⁸ Again, the devil took him to a very high mountain and showed him all the kingdoms of the world and their splendor. 9 "All this I will give you," he said, "if you will bow down and worship me."

¹⁰ Jesus said to him, "Away from me, Satan! For it is written: 'Worship the Lord your God, and serve him only.'"

¹¹ Then the devil left him, and angels came and attended him.

Before we discuss this Scripture, let's take a moment for each of us to reflect on our own.

- **What strikes you about Jesus' encounter with Satan? What questions does it raise for you?**

Jot down your thoughts in your participant guide.

Wait at least 1 minute—or even a little longer—so people can jot down their questions or thoughts before moving forward. This should be something that people do on their own—not in discussion groups. When it appears that everyone is ready to move on, continue.

GRAPPLING

We'll get to your questions and thoughts in a bit. But let's first grapple with a few other questions. Before we start into this time of discussion, let's remember that together we're creating a safe environment for sharing and conversation. This means we will all respect each other, listen to others before we jump in with our own thoughts, and welcome different opinions because they may bring us greater understanding in our own thoughts as well as the bigger picture. Let's trust that God will guide the direction we take as we explore the Bible together. Let's invite God to direct our conversation right now.

LESSON 2: CAN WE REALLY BEAT TEMPTATION? **21**

Pray for the group to be receptive to listening to each other and to hearing God. Commit the conversation to God, trusting him with every word, thought, and interaction. Ask God to direct the conversation where he wants it to go.

! LEADER LEARNING

Create a welcoming environment for all participants. As people share with the large group, be careful not to make it about "right and wrong" answers, which can hinder people from sharing their questions and uncertainties. Acknowledge responses with phrases such as "thanks for that insight" or "thanks for making us think" to encourage everyone to get involved and feel safe.

Let's start by discussing in our small groups. With your group, talk about the first two questions you'll find under the "Grappling" section of Lesson 2. You'll have about 8 minutes to talk through both questions—so plan your time accordingly.

- **Why do you think God allowed Jesus to be tempted by Satan?**

- **Why does Satan think he has any chance to persuade Jesus, the Son of God?**

Allow about 8 minutes for small group discussion. Then have each group share with the larger group something they feel is significant from either of the first two questions. Thank everyone for sharing.

Let's talk about this next question as a large group. As we grapple with this question, think back to how we responded to the everyday objects in the beginning of our time together.

- **What, if anything, did you discover about resisting temptation from Jesus' responses to temptation?**

Allow time for different people to share their thoughts with the whole group. Remember to model and encourage listening and respect for others as they share. When several people have had a chance to respond, continue.

Now that we've dug a little deeper, let's revisit some of the observations and question we jotted down on our own. Perhaps you have some new thoughts that came up throughout our discussion as well. Take about 10 minutes with your groups to share anything that seemed especially relevant, bewildering, or noteworthy to you as we read from Matthew 4. Help each other explore and grow.

Allow at least 10 minutes for groups

to talk. Give a 1-minute "time to wrap it up!" alert so groups have time to finish their thoughts.

I'd like to get a taste of what you talked about, and I'm sure others would too. What ideas or questions did your group discover in your discussion time together?

Allow a few minutes for different groups to share. Depending on how much time you have left you can simply let groups report their insights and questions, or if you have time you can invite the larger group to respond to an insight or question that was shared. Keep in mind some questions will go unanswered, and that's okay. God will continue to work in people even after they leave today's lesson.

BEHIND THE SCENES

James 1:13 says, "When tempted, no one should say, 'God is tempting me.' For God cannot be tempted by evil, nor does he tempt anyone." So how and why would God allow Jesus to be tempted? Remember, words we use slightly differ in meaning depending on the context and the translation. The word translated as "tempted" can also mean "tested." Some believe that Jesus could not sin, and others believe he chose not to sin. In any event, both Satan and the world needed tangible evidence of Jesus' success in dealing with Satan's temptations. The Bible was full of evidence of humans yielding to Satan's temptations before, but Jesus, God in human flesh, succeeded through the testing by knowing, believing, and applying God's Word.

Remember your "I-shouldn't-have-done-that" moment and what led up to it? Jesus' temptation turned out well—better than our "I-shouldn't-have-done-that" moments. What's the difference, besides the obvious one that Jesus is God and we are not? His life on earth is an example for us, so we need to wrestle through to consider what we need to glean from his life.

- **How can Jesus' life leading up to the time of testing, as well as the testing itself, help us when faced with temptations and tests in our own lives?**

Invite people to share their thoughts with the rest of the group. Be sure to thank people for being fearless in their conversation.

BEHIND THE SCENES

Jesus uses the words "it is written" three times in Matthew 4:1-11. In fact, Jesus quotes the Old Testament dozens of times in the Gospel of Matthew alone. And Jesus isn't the only one who knows Scripture. Even Satan quotes Psalm 91 in Matthew 4:6. While it's important to know God's Word, it's even more important to live by its guidance.

LESSON 2: CAN WE REALLY BEAT TEMPTATION?

Leader Guide

GROWING

It's great to have these conversations and really dig into what the Bible says. This helps us move into greater understanding of God and grow in our relationship with God. One way we see that growth is through applying what we've discovered to our lives. God intends us to learn from what we read; God teaches us about himself, and God teaches us about ourselves.

BEHIND THE SCENES

Compare what Satan quotes in Matthew 4:6 with the original words in Psalm 91:11-12.

"If you are the Son of God," he said, "throw yourself down. For it is written: 'He will command his angels concerning you, and they will lift you up in their hands, so that you will not strike your foot against a stone.'" (Matthew 4:6)

"For he will command his angels concerning you to guard you in all your ways; they will lift you up in their hands, so that you will not strike your foot against a stone." (Psalm 91:11-12)

What do you notice about Satan's use of Psalm 91:11-12?

Jesus was tempted in body, soul, and spirit. He was tempted to please his body in ways that God says he would provide instead. He was tempted to put God to the test, questioning who he is and what he says he can/cannot and should/should not do. He was tempted to set up idols, assuming power and self-importance.

Jesus did not do any miracle to stop the temptation. He responded only in a way that is also possible for you and for me. He responded as any human could—by choosing to trust God and the truth of God's Word.

What about you?

- **As you cope with temptations in your life, what are ways you can trust God and the truth of God's Word? What might that look like for you?**

Invite everyone to write their reflections in the space provided in their participant guides. Let them know there is one more question for them there as well—they should go ahead and read and reflect on that one too.

Allow time for people to adequately reflect and journal, then close with a prayer, thanking God that we can approach him and each other without fear and trust him to provide and guide through everyday life.

FEARLESS CONVERSATION: **WHY IS JESUS SO RADICAL?**

LESSON 3: WHAT DOES IT REALLY MEAN TO FOLLOW JESUS?

LEADER PREP

- Read the entire lesson ahead of time. Also read the corresponding pages in the Why Is Jesus So Radical? Participant Guide as there may be additional material provided there that will be helpful to you.

- Make yourself familiar with the "Behind the Scenes" boxes scattered throughout this lesson. If someone has a question, it's better to refer them to the guide than to provide the answer yourself. You'll help your group become comfortable with researching their own questions about the Bible when they are studying alone.

- Have a ruler available for every two people. If you cannot locate enough rulers, you can use wooden dowel rods, unsharpened pencils, Tinker Toy stick pieces, and so on. Just make sure the objects are of a uniform length.

- Pray. Lots.

GREETING

BEHIND THE SCENES

When we meet Jesus in Matthew 4:18, he's left Nazareth for Capernaum, and then he continues through Galilee. Verse 23 indicates he taught in synagogues and healed every sickness among the people. His ministry wasn't reserved for those who had the most teaching. It wasn't reserved for Jews. He reached beyond the expectations of others as he connected with the Gentiles. People from many surrounding areas reached out to him, trusting him to teach and heal (verse 25). Jerusalem and Judea were Jewish regions, while Decapolis was primarily Gentiles, and Galilee was a region with a mixture of Jews and Gentiles. Jesus attracted and ministered to them all. He walked among all classes of people. He healed every disease (verse 24). Jesus didn't meet people's expectations. He exceeded them.

How does this challenge the social boundaries of life today?

- Welcome everyone and be sure to introduce yourself.

- Be sure everyone has a copy of the participant guide.

- Let everyone know you'll be moving through Lesson 3 today, so they can find that section in their participant guide and use it to prompt them through today's lesson.

- Explain that there are many "Behind the Scenes" commentary notes throughout the lesson. These can be read by participants as they come to that section of the lesson—or people who want to plan ahead can read them during the week to be ready for the next lesson.

Then ask:

How's your reaction time? We're going to find out! Pair up with someone and grab a ruler (or other object you located beforehand, and adjust the instructions accordingly).

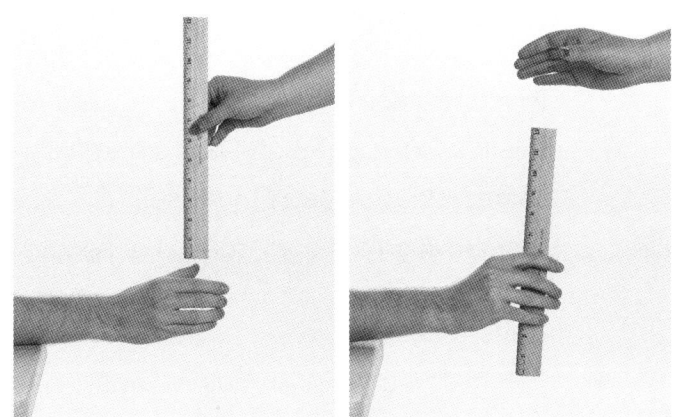

Here's how to test your reaction time. One person will sit or stand with his or her arm on a flat surface. Tables work great. The arm should be positioned so that the wrist extends just beyond the edge with the index finger and thumb positioned as if they're ready to clamp together and grab something—like a lobster claw. The other person will hold the ruler vertically above their partner's hand.

26   FEARLESS CONVERSATION: **WHY IS JESUS SO RADICAL?**

The end with zero on it should be just above your partner's finger and thumb, but make sure it's not touching. Without giving any other clues, such as eye contact, verbal warnings, and so on, the person with the ruler will drop it, and the partner should catch it as soon as possible. Write down the centimeter mark on the ruler where your finger and thumb clamp onto the ruler. (If you're using something other than a ruler, just have them write the approximate length of the place where they clasped the object—no need to be exact.)

There's space on page 23 in your participant guide to record your results. Repeat it three times, then switch so each person gets to test his or her reaction time. Make sure you introduce yourself to your partner, too.

Allow 5 minutes.

Get together with another pair, so you'll form a small group of four, introduce yourselves, and share what surprised—or didn't surprise— you about your reaction times. You'll have 4 minutes.

- **What suprised—or didn't surprise— you about your reaction time?**

Allow 4 minutes for people to get into small groups (they may need to move their chairs into smaller circles), introduce themselves, and discuss this question. Give them a 30 second "wrap-up" alert, and then continue.

Thanks for starting today with a challenge. We're going to continue the challenge as we grapple with questions about responding to people as we follow them. So, let's get started.

You'll find a question on page 23 of your participant guide. Discuss this with your small group for the next 5 minutes.

- **When you have the opportunity to lead, what do you expect of those who follow you?**

Allow 5 minutes for discussion. Give a 30-second wrap-up alert, then invite a few people to share their answer to the question with the larger group.

LEADER LEARNING

As a leader, you don't have to know (or share) all the answers. Learning is a process of the learner, and your role as a leader is to facilitate that process. Ask questions that guide the process. Invite people to explore. Give them space to process. Their questions and experiences won't match yours, but

God knows just where each of them—and you—are and where they need to go next. Trust God to reach a multitude of individuals with different needs even when they're all together in one room going through the same lesson.

GROUNDING

Let's get grounded in God's Word so we can understand more about what it means to follow Jesus. Today's Bible account is from Matthew 4:18-25. Jesus publicly begins his ministry following his baptism and time of testing in the wilderness. He moves from Nazareth to Capernaum and begins preaching. He then meets the people who will become his first disciples and begins to heal the sick.

Let's read Matthew's account.

Read Matthew 4:18-25 aloud, or ask for a volunteer from your group to read it aloud. Encourage everyone else to follow along in their own Bibles or in their participant guides.

God's Word: Matthew 4:18-25

¹⁸ As Jesus was walking beside the Sea of Galilee, he saw two brothers, Simon called Peter and his brother Andrew. They were casting a net into the lake, for they were fishermen. ¹⁹ "Come, follow me," Jesus said, "and I will send you out to fish for people." ²⁰ At once they left their nets and followed him.

²¹ Going on from there, he saw two other brothers, James son of Zebedee and his brother John. They were in a boat with their father Zebedee, preparing their nets. Jesus called them, ²² and immediately they left the boat and their father and followed him.

²³ Jesus went throughout Galilee, teaching in their synagogues, proclaiming the good news of the kingdom, and healing every disease and sickness among the people. ²⁴ News about him spread all over Syria, and people brought to him all who were ill with various diseases, those suffering severe pain, the demon-possessed, those having seizures, and the paralyzed; and he healed them. ²⁵ Large crowds from Galilee, the Decapolis, Jerusalem, Judea and the region across the Jordan followed him.

Before we discuss this, take a moment to personally reflect.

- **What are the first questions that come to mind about this passage? What sort of jumps out at you and catches your attention?**

Go ahead and capture those initial thoughts and questions in your participant guide.

Wait at least 1 minute—or even a little longer—so people can jot down their questions or thoughts before moving forward. This should be something that people do on their own—not in discussion groups. When it appears that everyone is ready to move on, continue.

GRAPPLING

We'll get to your personal questions and thoughts in a bit. Before we start into this time of discussion, I'd like to remind everyone that we want this to be a safe place to share our thoughts. This includes being respectful to each other and listening. Let's trust that God will guide the direction we take as we explore the Bible together.

BEHIND THE SCENES

Matthew 4:18-25 describes Jesus' calling of four men (Simon Peter, Andrew, James, and John) into ministry with him. Jesus didn't wait to see who would come to him. He met them where they were. Jesus didn't go to the Temple and get the experts of the Law to follow him. Jesus knew he needed people who could minister to, relate to, and provide for people in practical ways. He wanted people who could fish, as these men could. He promised them he'd teach them a different kind of fishing, but he would build on what they already knew to develop them into the disciples he knew they could be.

Let's start by discussing in our small groups. You'll find two questions under the "Grappling" section in your participant guide. Start with just the first one. You'll talk about this for 5 minutes or so in your small group.

- **As you read this passage from Matthew, how would you describe the way the disciples followed Jesus?**

Allow 5 minutes for discussion, then ask for a few people to share their observations with the larger group before moving on to the next question.

Let's talk about the next question as a large group. As we grapple with this question, keep your experience with the ruler and your reaction times in mind.

LESSON 3: WHAT DOES IT REALLY MEAN TO FOLLOW JESUS?

Leader Guide

- **When Jesus calls followers today, does he expect them to react by dropping everything immediately and following him on the spot? Explain your answer.**

Allow 5 to 8 minutes for large group sharing. Remember to model and encourage listening and respect for others as they share. Thank everyone for sharing.

Now that we've dug a little deeper, let's revisit some of the observations and question we jotted down on our own. Maybe you have some new ones that came up during our discussion as well. Take about 10 minutes with your groups to share anything that seemed especially relevant, bewildering, or noteworthy to you as we read from Matthew 4. We'll help each other explore and grow.

Allow at least 10 minutes for groups to talk. Give a 1-minute alert so groups have time to finish their thoughts.

I'd like to get a taste of what you talked about, and I'm sure others would too! Does any group want to share an insight that your group found interesting?

Allow a few minutes for different groups to share. Depending on how much time you have left, you can simply let groups report their insights and questions, or if you have time you can invite the larger group to respond to an insight or question that was shared. Keep in mind some questions will go unanswered, and that's okay. God will continue to work in people even after they leave today's lesson.

LEADER LEARNING

Bringing the large group together for brief sharing after small group discussions helps participants glean ideas and insights from those outside their small group. While it's necessary to keep most discussions within a small group experience—for time constraints, trust, and relationships—bringing the large group back together for a "taste test" of responses provides variety and enthusiasm.

BEHIND THE SCENES

This wasn't the first experience Andrew and Simon Peter had with Jesus. Andrew was one of John the Baptist's disciples who encountered Jesus as John identified him as the Lamb of God (John 1:35-40). The first thing Andrew did was tell his brother, Simon Peter, and take him to Jesus, where Simon Peter had his first interaction with Jesus (John 1:41-42).

There are two primary words translated into "know" in our English Bibles. One (*ginōskō*) indicates an insight, awareness, and understanding. It's what God gives us. We might not be aware of every bit of knowledge he's given us, but it's something we don't have to actively learn or experience. He gifts it to us, and it's as if we know it by intuition. The other kind of knowing (*nous*) is what we acquire by learning. We have to experience it somehow—through hearing, reading, doing, and so on—in order to gain the knowledge. Just because we know *about* Jesus doesn't mean we *know* Jesus.

How do you know him?

After Jesus called his disciples and they responded immediately by following him, Jesus proceeded to continue ministering to people throughout Galilee, teaching, proclaiming, and healing.

• **What does the variety of Jesus' actions and interactions in Matthew 4:18-25 tell you about his ministry—and what it might look like for you to follow Jesus?**

Invite people to share their thoughts with the rest of the group. Be sure to thank people for being fearless in their conversation.

GROWING

It's great to have these conversations and really dig into what the Bible says. This helps us move into greater understanding of God and grow in our relationship with God. One way we see that growth is through applying what we've discovered to our lives. God intends us to learn from what we read; he teaches us about himself, and he teaches us about ourselves.

BEHIND THE SCENES

When Jesus commanded Simon Peter, Andrew, James, and John to follow him, it wasn't a passive invitation. They left what they knew to follow who they wanted to know. Jesus wouldn't just teach them what he knew; he taught them who he was. Following him involved more than accompanying him; it required sacrifice and commitment. It required setting themselves aside and emulating Jesus.

"Then he said to them all: 'Whoever wants to be my disciple must deny themselves and take up their cross daily and follow me. For whoever wants to save their life will lose it, but whoever loses their life for me will save it'" (Luke 9:23-24).

BEHIND THE SCENES

Matthew tells us that the first disciples immediately followed Jesus when he called them. But that immediate response to Jesus' calling didn't mean that they followed him without questions or problems. Far from it. In fact, the Gospels indicate that the disciples wrestled with their commitment, even after Jesus' resurrection from death. Even at the end of Matthew, the 11 remaining disciples

LESSON 3: WHAT DOES IT REALLY MEAN TO FOLLOW JESUS? 31

Leader Guide

went to the mountain where Jesus told them to meet him. When they got there, "they worshipped him; but some doubted" (Matthew 28:17). Nonetheless, Jesus commissioned the disciples to go and make disciples of all nations.

How has a mixture of belief and doubt marked your own discipleship?

Let's revisit our reaction time experience and try it again. But this time we'll add a new element. The person who is dropping the ruler will give their partner a clue about when he or she will drop the ruler. The person dropping the ruler decides what it will be. It might be a simple sound, such as a snap or phrase, or it might be a 3-2-1 countdown. It's up to the person dropping the ruler to decide. Let your partner know what it is and try it a couple times, recording reaction times. Then switch places, again letting the person dropping the ruler decide what the clue will be. Once you've recorded two reaction times for each person, rejoin your small group of four and briefly share your experience.

- **How has your reaction time changed, and why?**

Allow about 5 minutes, giving a 1-minute alert. Then continue.

Following Jesus requires knowing Jesus. Knowing Jesus includes taking time for a relationship with him and looking to him for leadership. As the disciples model for us, following requires a response. Consider your reaction time to God.

- **How would you describe your reaction time to God? What influences how quickly you respond to God?**

Invite everyone to write their reflections in the space provided in their participant guides. Let them know there is one more question for them there as well—they should go ahead and read and reflect on that one too.

Allow time for people to adequately reflect and journal, then close with a prayer, thanking God that we can approach him and each other without fear and trust him to provide and guide through everyday life.

32 FEARLESS CONVERSATION: **WHY IS JESUS SO RADICAL?**

FEARLESS CONVERSATION

LESSON 4: HOW CAN I TELL IF JESUS CARES ENOUGH TO ACT IN MY SITUATION?

LEADER PREP

- Read the entire lesson ahead of time. Also read the corresponding pages in the Why Is Jesus So Radical? Participant Guide as there may be additional material provided there that will be helpful to you.

- You'll find "Behind the Scenes" boxes with Bible commentary provided throughout this lesson. They're there to help you gain a better understanding of the Bible. The people in your group with have these too.

- Pray. Lots.

GREETING

- Welcome everyone and be sure to introduce yourself.

- Be sure everyone has a copy of the participant guide.

- Let everyone know you'll be moving through Lesson 4 today, so they can find that section in the guide and use it to prompt them through today's lesson.

- Explain that there are many "Behind the Scenes" commentary notes throughout the lesson. These can be read by participants as they come to that section of the lesson—or people who want to plan ahead can read

LESSON 4: HOW CAN I TELL IF JESUS CARES ENOUGH TO ACT IN MY SITUATION? 33 them during the week to be ready for the next lesson.

Then ask:

Tell about someone you saw this past week who seemed to need help. Maybe it was a person who was homeless and looking for change or a friend needing a job. What was the situation and what—if anything—did you do to get involved?

Let several people share with the large group.

LEADER LEARNING

Sharing among a large group can be tricky, because you never know how long or how much people will share. Remember, as a leader, you're helping the entire group learn, and if one person is allowed to dominate the time, few people are learning. Watch for clues that someone might be on the verge of oversharing. Gently interject a comment such as, "We'll have more time to share details within our small groups, but let's keep our large group comments brief for time's sake" or "Thanks for sharing. I want to make sure to allow for a few more comments."

Thanks for your comments. The world is full of needs and we can't respond to all of them. But we do expect people to respond to our needs, don't we? Today we're talking about whether we can count on Jesus to meet our needs. But before we dive into that, let's talk about this:

- **Who's a person who has stepped up and met a need of yours? Maybe it was a physical need, an emotional one, or even a financial one. Who was it, and what did that person do for you?**

Let's get into smaller groups and talk about it. Find a group of four people and discuss the question. Make sure you introduce yourselves too. You'll have 4 minutes.

Allow about 4 minutes for people to get into small groups (they may need to move their chairs into smaller circles), introduce themselves, and discuss the question, which they'll find in their participant guides. Give them a 30-second "wrap-up" alert, then continue.

Thanks for sharing in your groups and getting to know each other a little better. Today we're going to grapple with questions related to whether or not people—or God—care about our situations, and how they show that they care. Has it ever happened that you have seen a need in someone's life, but you decided not to take

action because you believed that was actually the better way to help the person? For example, you might have seen a toddler struggling to get a spoon in her mouth. Instead of doing that task for her, you purposely did not help, knowing that she would learn through the struggle.

- **When have you seen a need in someone's life—but decided not to take action because you believed that was actually the better way to help the person?**

Talk about that in your small group.

Allow 4 minutes for discussion. Give groups a 30-second alert, and then invite a few people to share their thoughts with the entire group.

We can see that there are a variety of responses available to us when we see someone in need. And even in our own situations of need we may desire one outcome but there could be other options. Keep that in mind as we continue.

GROUNDING

Let's get grounded in God's Word so we can understand more about how Jesus cares for us. Today's Bible account is from Matthew 9:18-26. Let's read Matthew's account.

Read Matthew 9:18-26 aloud, or ask for a volunteer from your group to read it aloud. Encourage everyone else to follow along in their own Bibles or in their participant guides.

God's Word: Matthew 9:18-26

18 While he was saying this, a synagogue leader came and knelt before him and said, "My daughter has just died. But come and put your hand on her, and she will live." 19 Jesus got up and went with him, and so did his disciples.

20 Just then a woman who had been subject to bleeding for twelve years came up behind him and touched the edge of his cloak. 21 She said to herself, "If I only touch his cloak, I will be healed."

22 Jesus turned and saw her. "Take heart, daughter," he said, "your faith has healed you." And the woman was healed at that moment.

LEADER GUIDE

> ²³ When Jesus entered the synagogue leader's house and saw the noisy crowd and people playing pipes, ²⁴ he said, "Go away. The girl is not dead but asleep." But they laughed at him. ²⁵ After the crowd had been put outside, he went in and took the girl by the hand, and she got up. ²⁶ News of this spread through all that region.

Before we discuss this, take a moment to personally reflect.

- **What are the first questions that come to mind? What jumps out at you and catches your attention?**

Capture those initial thoughts and questions in your participant guide.

Wait at least 1 minute—or even a little longer—so people can jot down their questions or thoughts before moving forward. This should be something that people do on their own—not in discussion groups. When it appears that everyone is ready to move on, continue.

GRAPPLING

We'll get to your personal questions and thoughts in a bit, but I have a few questions for us first. And before we jump into those, I want to remind us all that this conversation is one that's open to everyone. Throughout our time let's be respectful of each other and listen to others before we jump in with our own thoughts. We can also trust that God is here and is part of this conversation. God is big enough to guide us!

BEHIND THE SCENES

Matthew 9:18-26 describes two healings Jesus performs. One is of a woman suffering from a bleeding condition; and the other is the young daughter of a synagogue leader named Jairus. The woman pursues and reaches out to touch Jesus. Jesus goes to the young girl's house and touches her (after her father pursues Jesus). One doesn't have to say a word; the other explains the situation requiring healing. Both the bleeding woman and Jairus display faith that Jesus can heal. Nothing is mentioned about the faith of the young girl herself.

In your small group, talk about the first two questions you'll find under the "Grappling" section in your participant guide. You'll have about 8 minutes to discuss these.

- **What similarities and what differences do you observe in these healings?**

36 FEARLESS CONVERSATION: **WHY IS JESUS SO RADICAL?**

• **What do you discover about Jesus through these two accounts?**

Allow 8 minutes for discussion; then have several groups share one or two of their insights.

Now that we've dug a little deeper, let's revisit some of the observations and question we jotted down on our own, as well as any new questions that may have come up. Take about 10 minutes with your groups to share anything that seemed especially relevant, bewildering, or noteworthy to you as we read from Matthew 9. We'll help each other explore and grow.

Allow at least 10 minutes for groups to talk. Give a 1-minute "time to wrap it up!" alert so groups have time to finish their thoughts.

Let's hear what you talked about in your small groups. Does any group want to share an idea or a question that your group found interesting?

Allow a few minutes for different groups to share. Depending on how much time you have left you can simply let groups report their insights and questions, or if you have time you can invite the larger group to respond to an insight or question that was shared. Keep in mind some questions will go unanswered, and that's okay. God will continue to work in people even after they leave today's lesson.

BEHIND THE SCENES

A woman who had a bleeding condition would have been considered unclean under Mosaic law, as a woman was considered unclean any time she was bleeding, including a regular menstrual cycle.

"When a woman has a discharge of blood for many days at a time other than her monthly period or has a discharge that continues beyond her period, she will be unclean as long as she has the discharge, just as in the days of her period. Any bed she lies on while her discharge continues will be unclean, as is her bed during her monthly period, and anything she sits on will be unclean, as during her period. Anyone who touches them will be unclean; they must wash their clothes and bathe with water, and they will be unclean till evening. When she is cleansed from her discharge, she must count off seven days, and after that she will be ceremonially clean" (Leviticus 15:25-28).

An ongoing bleeding condition would have isolated a woman from all regular contact from people, including justifying divorce by her husband. If someone entered the Temple while unclean, the penalty could range from forty lashes to death by stoning.

Mark's account of this woman adds a detail: "She had suffered a great deal under the care

LESSON 4: HOW CAN I TELL IF JESUS CARES ENOUGH TO ACT IN MY SITUATION?

LEADER GUIDE

of many doctors and had spent all she had, yet instead of getting better she grew worse" (Mark 5:26). Suffice it to say, she was chronically suffering and desperately wanted healing.

How have you experienced a desperate need for healing—physically, emotionally, relationally, or financially?

We read Jesus' comments on the woman's faith (verse 22), and we see the synagogue leader's faith in his pursuit of Jesus and belief that his daughter will live with Jesus' touch. We also see people's doubt in verses 23 and 24: "When Jesus entered the synagogue leader's house and saw the noisy crowd and people playing pipes, he said, 'Go away. The girl is not dead but asleep.' But they laughed at him." Faith and doubt live side-by-side—even within us at times. I realize this will take some boldness from each of us, but I'd like us to be fearless and talk about how this relates to our own lives.

- **How have you experienced faith and doubt side by side?**

Allow about 5 minutes for conversation, giving a 30-second "wrap it up" comment as needed. Then continue.

BEHIND THE SCENES

When Jesus arrives at the synagogue leader Jairus' home, there is a crowd, including people playing pipes, which indicates mourning for the girl is well underway. This isn't a crowd sitting in an intensive care waiting room, fervently praying for a miraculous recovery. This is a funeral home crowd. Jesus' reference to the girl sleeping doesn't indicate a lack of death, as if the mourners don't know the difference between someone who is alive and someone who is dead.

Jesus is referring to a state also referred to in 1 Thessalonians 4:13-14: "Brothers and sisters, we do not want you to be uninformed about those who sleep in death, so that you do not grieve like the rest of mankind, who have no hope. For we believe that Jesus died and rose again, and so we believe that God will bring with Jesus those who have fallen asleep in him."

This type of sleep looks like death to us but is the same state from which believers will be awakened at the time of the final resurrection.

LEADER LEARNING

When we invite fearless conversation, there will be some uncomfortable moments, such as when people believe different things about what the Bible teaches. It's okay for people to wrestle with God to reach truth. Of course, we want all discussions to include respect for one another, but respect and agreement aren't the same thing. Avoid any tendencies you might have for wrapping everything up in a neat bow

38 FEARLESS CONVERSATION: **WHY IS JESUS SO RADICAL?**

and making sure everything is neat and tidy before the lesson ends. Tolerate some tension, because it often gives us space to grow.

"As iron sharpens iron, so one person sharpens another." (Proverbs 27:17)

GROWING

It's great to have these conversations and really dig into what the Bible says. This helps us move into greater understanding of God and to grow in our relationship with God. One way we see that growth is through applying what we've discovered to our lives. God intends us to learn from what we read; he teaches us about himself, and he teaches us about ourselves.

BEHIND THE SCENES

The story of Jairus and his daughter is also found in the book of Mark, which can give us a little extra insight into the story.

When Jairus first comes to Jesus, his daughter is in the process of dying. Jesus goes with him (Mark 5:22-24). That's when the woman with the bleeding condition, among a large crowd, presses toward him, reaches him, and is healed. Keep in mind that Jairus is still with Jesus. He sees throngs of people slowing Jesus down. He sees Jesus turn around to ask, "Who touched my clothes?" More time passes as Jesus "kept looking around to see who had done it" (Mark 5:32). The woman explains to Jesus that it was her, and they have a conversation. Time continues to pass, and Jairus is still with Jesus when people come to tell him his daughter has died: "'Your daughter is dead,' they said. 'Why bother the teacher anymore?' Overhearing what they said, Jesus told him, 'Don't be afraid; just believe' " (Mark 5:35-36).

Jairus may have thought he'd run out of time, but he hadn't. Still, he had a choice whether or not to continue to believe. He could have gotten angry at the woman who interrupted Jesus' travel to his house. Jairus could have questioned Jesus' intentions for going with him in the first place if Jesus was willing to get delayed by someone else who needed healing. He could have questioned whether or not Jesus cared enough about him to heal his daughter. But Jairus chose to believe instead.

Jesus provided healing for the bleeding woman and Jairus' daughter. And we really don't know exactly why God chooses to heal some and not others—as is our experience in life today. It may be related to God's greater knowledge of the scope of our lives, just as we shared earlier that there are times we don't act to help someone because of a valid reason, which we know but the other person may not know. God does know, and we have to trust in that. It's hard though!

The people we read about in the Bible today believed Jesus could and would heal. But belief and healing—at least, the way we expect it—don't always go hand in hand. Belief isn't just about believing in what Jesus can do; it also means believing in who he is and what he wills.

Before we reflect on our final questions today, let's pray together as small groups. You've heard people in your small group share pieces of their lives. Take the next 3 to 4 minutes to pray for and with each other. When you're done, privately read the final questions in your participant guide and write your thoughts. I believe God will honor our fearless conversation—with each other and with him. You're then free to leave—thank you for joining us for fearless conversation today, and please come back next time for more.

As small groups wrap up their prayer time, they'll write personal reflections to the final questions in their participant guides:

- **What have I discovered today about knowing if Jesus cares enough to act in my situation? How am I going to respond in fearless faith today?**

- **As we move through this quarter, we'll contually be wondering on the question, Why is Jesus so radical? Based only on what we've discussed today, what's one sentence that might answer that question?**

Because we're ending today's lesson with a quiet, reflective tone, people might quietly leave. If you notice the volume in the room begin to rise while others are still reflecting, personally approach people to ask them to keep the room free of distractions for those who need it. You might also notice people who need additional attention; when possible, redirect another small group member to help them. Trust God to provide the healing most needed.

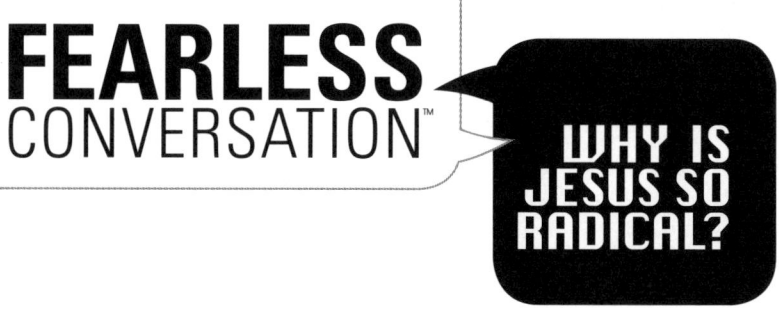

LESSON 5:
WHAT DOES IT MEAN IF JESUS REALLY IS GOD'S SON?

LEADER PREP

- Read the entire lesson ahead of time. Also read the corresponding pages in the Why Is Jesus So Radical? Participant Guide as there may be additional material provided there that will be helpful to you.

- You'll find "Behind the Scenes" boxes with Bible commentary provided throughout this lesson. They're there to help you gain a better understanding of the Bible. The people in your group will have these too.

- Pray. Lots.

FOR EXTRA IMPACT

Find a story or video clip about an exceptional child and provide a way to watch this either with a computer, tablet, or other devise. If you need an idea, look up video clips on YouTube about Emily Bear, a 6-year-old piano prodigy.

Prep Notes:
_____
_____
_____

GREETING

Leader Guide

- Welcome everyone and be sure to introduce yourself.

- Be sure everyone has a copy of the participant guide.

- Let everyone know you'll be moving through Lesson 5 today, so they can find that section in the guide and use this to prompt them through today's lesson.

- Explain that there are many "Behind the Scenes" commentary notes throughout the lesson. These can be read by participants as they come to that section of the lesson—or people who want to plan ahead can read them during the week to be ready for the next lesson.

Then ask:

What's your secret talent or ability? Can you cook like a world-class chef? Can you do backflips? Are you a member of a clowning club? I'll let you know my secret talent, it's... Briefly share a talent or ability you have. Model the kind of sharing you'd like people to do during this lesson. **Now it's your turn. What's your secret talent or ability?**

Let people call out their talents/dream talents. You can even have a few demonstrations.

Let's get into smaller groups and talk a little more. Get into groups of no more than four, and answer this question:

- **Even if you don't have what you might consider to be a special talent, what makes you unique?**

Talk about that in your small group. Be sure you introduce yourselves too!

Allow about 4 minutes for people to get into small groups (they may need to move their chairs into smaller circles), introduce themselves, and discuss this question. After about 4 minutes have everyone return their attention to you.

Thanks for sharing in your groups and getting to know each other a little better. Today we're going to be grappling with questions related to Jesus as God's Son—and the interesting way three disciples discovered his "true identity."

Now I have a discussion topic for you and your group.

FEARLESS CONVERSATION: **WHY IS JESUS SO RADICAL?**

If you have brought a way to share a video clip about an exceptional child, share this now before leading into this next section. If you have not brought this, continue with the lesson.

Consider how your life would be different if you found out that your child (or a child you love, such as a niece or nephew or the child of a close friend) was a musical prodigy. What if he was a math prodigy? Or what if she could hit a golf ball 300 yards at 8 years of age? How might your life be different? How might the child's life be different? What challenges might they (and you) face? What are some of the potential joys in such a situation? How would your life be different once faced with that knowledge? You'll have about 4 minutes.

- **How would life be different if an important child in your life was a prodigy?**

Let groups talk together and come up with thoughts on how their lives would be different. Then call everyone's attention back to you. Invite a few groups to share from their discussions. Then continue.

Most parents find reasons to be proud of their children, even if those kids are not prodigies. We all know someone who loves to brag about their child. But imagine what it would be like to be Mary and Joseph, raising Jesus and thinking, "This kid is God's Son!" Or to have the one and only God say about Jesus, "This is my Son, and I'm proud of him." Wow! That really is something worth bragging about! We're going to be digging into an account in the Bible where God says this very thing.

GROUNDING

Let's get grounded in God's Word so we can understand more about the radical way God communicated with us through Jesus. Today's Bible account is from Luke 9:18-36. Let's read what he's recorded for us.

Read Luke 9:18-36 aloud, or ask for a volunteer from your group to read it aloud. Encourage everyone else to follow along in their own Bibles or in their participant guides.

LESSON 5: WHAT DOES IT MEAN IF JESUS REALLY IS GOD'S SON?

God's Word: Luke 9:18-36

[18] Once when Jesus was praying in private and his disciples were with him, he asked them, "Who do the crowds say I am?"

[19] They replied, "Some say John the Baptist; others say Elijah; and still others, that one of the prophets of long ago has come back to life."

[20] "But what about you?" he asked. "Who do you say I am?"

Peter answered, "God's Messiah."

[21] Jesus strictly warned them not to tell this to anyone. [22] And he said, "The Son of Man must suffer many things and be rejected by the elders, the chief priests and the teachers of the law, and he must be killed and on the third day be raised to life."

[23] Then he said to them all: "Whoever wants to be my disciple must deny themselves and take up their cross daily and follow me. [24] For whoever wants to save their life will lose it, but whoever loses their life for me will save it. [25] What good is it for someone to gain the whole world, and yet lose or forfeit their very self? [26] Whoever is ashamed of me and my words, the Son of Man will be ashamed of them when he comes in his glory and in the glory of the Father and of the holy angels.

[27] "Truly I tell you, some who are standing here will not taste death before they see the kingdom of God."

[28] About eight days after Jesus said this, he took Peter, John and James with him and went up onto a mountain to pray. [29] As he was praying, the appearance of his face changed, and his clothes became as bright as a flash of lightning. [30] Two men, Moses and Elijah, appeared in glorious splendor, talking with Jesus. [31] They spoke about his departure, which he was about to bring to fulfillment at Jerusalem. [32] Peter and his companions were very sleepy, but when they became fully awake, they saw his glory and the two men standing with him. [33] As the men were leaving Jesus, Peter said to him, "Master, it is good for us to be here. Let us put up three shelters—one for you, one for Moses and one for Elijah." (He did not know what he was saying.)

[34] While he was speaking, a cloud appeared and covered them, and they were afraid as they entered the cloud. [35] A voice came from the cloud, saying, "This is my Son, whom I have chosen; listen to him." [36] When the voice had spoken, they found that Jesus was alone. The disciples kept this to themselves and did not tell anyone at that time what they had seen.

Before we discuss this I'd like you to take a moment to reflect.

- **What are the first questions and thoughts that come to mind about this passage?**

Go ahead and write down your initial thoughts and questions in your participant guide.

Wait at least 1 minute—or even a little longer—so people can jot down their questions or thoughts before moving forward. This should be something that people do on their own—not in discussion groups. When it appears that everyone is ready to move on, continue.

GRAPPLING

We'll get to your personal questions and thoughts in a bit. But let's grapple with a few other questions first. Before we start into this time of discussion, let's remember that together we're creating a safe environment for sharing and conversation. This means we will all respect each other, listen to others before we jump in with our own thoughts, and welcome different opinions because they may bring us to greater understanding. Also, we believe that God is here and part of this conversation. We can trust that God can guide the direction we take as we explore the Bible together. So let's invite God to direct our conversation right now!

Pray for the group to be open to hearing each other and hearing God. Ask God to open hearts to be receptive to each other—and ask God to direct the conversation to the place it needs to go.

LEADER LEARNING

Now as we really dig in, don't worry if things wander a little. Insights rarely follow a straight line. It's possible that God may be directing the conversation to an area that will have even greater impact on the lives of those in your group than you could imagine. In fact, it's often not the questions and answers themselves that help us grow, but the examination of those questions and answers in God's presence and the input of those around us that allows us to gain insight.

BEHIND THE SCENES

Luke 9:18-36 represents a major turning point in both Jesus' teaching and the disciples' understanding of who Jesus really is. With Peter's answer to the question, "Who do the crowds say I am?" the question of Jesus' underlying identity is revealed, and

LESSON 5: WHAT DOES IT MEAN IF JESUS REALLY IS GOD'S SON? 45

LEADER GUIDE

Jesus' focus shifts to preparing the disciples for his coming death and their changing responsibilities. In fact, Jesus references his impending suffering six times in Luke (9:22, 44; 12:50; 13:31-33; 17:25; 18:31). Three of the references also have parallels in Mark 8:31-32, 9:30-32, and 10:32-34 (the other three references are unique to Luke's Gospel).

At this point the disciples think this revelation about Jesus and the kingdom of God means there will be an immediate victory. Jesus will have to show the disciples that long before there is a final victory, he must face death on the cross and they will have to adopt lives of sacrificial service. To reiterate this point, the voice from heaven at the place of the Transfiguration tells them to listen to Jesus because he knows the true way to God.

Let's start by discussing in our small groups. As a group, talk about the first question you'll find under the "Grappling" section in your participant guide.

- **If we're honest, we usually think about Jesus as the nice man from the pictures tacked to the wall of our Sunday school rooms. If you were asked the question Jesus asked his followers in Luke 9:20, how would you answer?**

You'll talk about this for about 5 minutes in your small group, and then we'll hear some reports back to the larger group.

Allow 5 minutes for discussion, and then have each group share something they feel is significant. Thank everyone for sharing.

Let's talk about this next question as a large group.

- **What is the significance of Jesus' transfiguration? Why didn't Jesus just come out and tell the disciples who he was from the start?**

Allow time for different people to share their thoughts with the whole group. Remember to model and encourage listening and respect for others as they share. When several people have had a chance to respond, continue.

BEHIND THE SCENES

This was not the only time Jesus shared such a powerful experience with Peter, James, and John. The first time was when he raised Jairus' daughter from the dead (Luke 8:51; Mark 5:37), and the other time was in the Garden of Gethsemane just before his arrest (Mark 14:33). So it was no accident that Jesus selected these particular disciples to witness his transfiguration. Not only were they three of Jesus' closest friends, but they actually understood more of Jesus' mission and the essence of who he was than anyone else.

So far we've looked at this event through the questions and information offered in the material. Now, take a few minutes to share in your groups about your own observations and questions. What things were especially relevant to you as we read from this portion of Luke? Discuss that with your groups and share whatever questions popped into your mind. This is your time to dig into the things that made an impact on you if you're willing to tackle them.

Allow at least 10 minutes for groups to talk. Give a 1-minute warning so groups have time to finish their discussions.

Let's hear from a few groups. Who would be willing to share an idea or a question that your group found interesting?

Allow a few minutes for different groups to share. Depending on how much time you have left you can simply let groups report their insights and questions, or if you have time you can invite the larger group to respond to an insight or question that was shared. Then continue.

LEADER LEARNING

If you don't have all the answers, don't worry. It's okay to leave some things unresolved. As Paul says in 1 Corinthians 4:1, "This, then, is how you ought to regard us: as servants of Christ and as those entrusted with the mysteries God has revealed." Not every question will have a simple answer (in fact, most won't!), but this is a chance to invite people to participate in the process of exploration. If there are questions that don't have answers, you can encourage people to dig into these more afterward—these might be great opportunities for continued discussion over coffee later in the week.

You may have heard or even said the phrase, "I had a mountain-top experience." This expression usually describes an experience (spiritual or otherwise) that leaves us feeling inspired, exhilarated, or illuminated. Sometimes these experiences are life-altering and they leave us changed forever. But there are other times we have what we would call a mountain-top experience that is actually little more than excitement brought on by the moment. Sometimes an experience during a retreat, a revival, or a concert leaves us with a temporary "high" that fades almost as quickly as it arrives. How can we know the difference?

Invite people to share their thoughts with the rest of the group.

LESSON 5: WHAT DOES IT MEAN IF JESUS REALLY IS GOD'S SON?

LEADER GUIDE

BEHIND THE SCENES

It is significant that the Transfiguration took place on a mountain. Many other powerful biblical events took place on mountains. God told Abraham to take his son Isaac to one of the mountains in the region of Moriah and sacrifice him (Genesis 22:2). Moses received the Ten Commandments on Mount Sinai. Elijah the prophet found God's reassuring presence on the same mountain in a "gentle whisper" (1 Kings 19:12). Jesus commissioned the disciples on a mountain. Jesus delivered his most famous sermon on a mountain. In fact, the Gospel of Matthew lists six significant mountain events: Jesus' temptation (4:8); the Sermon on the Mount (5:1); numerous healings (15:29-30); the Transfiguration (17:1); Jesus' foretelling of the destruction of the Temple and the signs of the end times (24:1); and the commissioning of the disciples (28:16).

GROWING

We often talk about a visible and an invisible world. The physical world and the spiritual world. In Luke 9:18-36, Jesus' closest and most trusted friends were shown something of the spiritual world that came straight from heaven. And as if to seal it, God instructed, "This is my Son, whom I have chosen; listen to him."

God's voice actually served two purposes. First, it was an affirmation of Christ as God's Son. Second, it was a reminder to the disciples that they were talking too much and thinking too little. They were responding to the physical situation more than they were the spiritual truth behind it.

What about you? Have you ever had a "mountain-top experience"? Can you think of a time in your life when you have felt the presence of God in a powerful way? How did you react? Were you moved to action, or did you want to stay in the presence of God and let the feeling be enough? Let's talk about this in our groups.

- When have you had a "mountain-top experience" where you felt God in a powerful way? How did you react?

Allow 5 minutes for discussion, and then have people return their attention to you.

BEHIND THE SCENES

Jesus' refusal of Peter's desire to build a tabernacle is more than just a reaction to the disciple's exuberance. It is a tangible reminder that revelation and inspiration have a purpose. They are to be demonstrated in both inward reflection and outward acts of ministry and service.

In this account in Luke, the disciples are faced with a dilemma. They are moving from an intellectual understanding of Jesus as the Son of God to a deeper spiritual understanding of the same thing. The idea of a living Messiah is no longer a concept. In some ways they have met the Son of God in the flesh for the first time. Jesus gives them an idea of what this is going to mean for their lives—and for his own life as well.

Let's take time to reflect on what meeting Jesus as the Messiah, as God's Son, means for us personally. There are two last questions in your book. Reflect on those privately, journaling your thoughts.

- **If Jesus is the Messiah, God's Son, what does that mean for my life?**

- **This quarter we're grappling with the question, Why is Jesus so radical? Based only on what we've discussed today, what's one sentence that might answer that question?**

Allow time for people to adequately reflect and journal; then close with a prayer, thanking God that we can approach him and each other without fear.

BEHIND THE SCENES

The Transfiguration is a moment full of mystery and supernatural phenomena, with the voice speaking from the cloud (a biblical symbol for God). That's interesting because of its imagery. After the exodus from Egypt, a cloud led the Israelites on their journey to the Promised Land. And in Acts when Jesus ascended to heaven, he did so through a cloud.

Leader Guide

LESSON 5: WHAT DOES IT MEAN IF JESUS REALLY IS GOD'S SON?

FEARLESS CONVERSATION

WHY IS JESUS SO RADICAL?

LESSON 6:
WHY DID JESUS TELL SUCH CONFUSING STORIES?

LEADER PREP

- Read the entire lesson ahead of time. Also read the corresponding pages in the Why Is Jesus So Radical? Participant Guide as there may be additional material provided there that will be helpful to you.

- You'll find "Behind the Scenes" boxes with Bible commentary provided throughout this lesson. They're there to help you gain a better understanding of the Bible. The people in your group will have these too.

- Bring an object from home that has sentimental value to you, and be ready to briefly tell the story behind the object and what this item says about you. For example: "This pocket knife is special because it was a gift from my grandfather, and he enjoyed carving. Every time I use it, I am reminded of the wonderful toys he carved with it, and I have taken up the hobby of whittling myself."

- Pray. Lots.

Prep Notes:

GREETING

LEADER GUIDE

BEHIND THE SCENES

The parables (and corresponding concepts) in Matthew 13:24-45 were a departure from the norm for the people of Jesus' day. He was using a new form of communication to deliver a new kind of message; something very different from what they were accustomed to hearing. These were stories that engaged the people listening in every aspect of their lives. And they were *secular* stories. Stories about land, livestock, treasures, money, food, occupations. Things the people understood. But the amazing thing is that these stories were designed to move the listener from a world they were familiar with to a world filled with hope and promise. A world where peace and justice were the standard.

For example, in the parable of the weeds, Jesus talked about a world they were familiar with: The world of agriculture. But in talking about a sower who scattered his seeds in a field (just as many of them had done themselves), the emphasis moves subtly from the day-to-day trials of a farmer to the reality of two kingdoms set squarely against one another. And it leaves the hearer with a question: *What kind of seed am I?*

Parables were a stark reminder that the things the people had grown comfortable with were not necessarily trustworthy and sometimes our efforts to right a wrong simply make things worse (pulling the wheat with the weeds). And by following God's direction we see that evil is temporary and good ultimately endures.

- Welcome everyone and be sure to introduce yourself.

- Be sure everyone has a copy of the participant guide.

- Let everyone know you'll be moving through Lesson 6 today, so they can find that section in the guide and use this it prompt them through today's lesson.

- Explain that there are many "Behind the Scenes" commentary notes throughout the lesson. These can be read by participants as they come to that section of the lesson—or people who want to plan ahead can read them during the week to be ready for the next lesson.

Then ask:

Okay, let's jump off the page, so to speak. Get into a group with three other people, and share a short story about your life that we wouldn't find on your resume or your Facebook page. It could be something strange that happened this week, something funny that happened on a vacation, or any other story about you that you can tell in 1 minute. And be sure to share your name!

Allow about a minute for people to get into small groups, and then 4 more minutes for them to share their stories. Give a 30-second "time to wrap it up!" warning, and then have everyone turn their attention back to you.

It's fun to hear stories and to get to know each other a bit. Let's talk about stories and why they have meaning in our lives. In your group use the first question in the "Greeting" section to dig into this a bit.

- **Why are stories—about our lives or anything else—important?**

Allow about 4 minutes for people to discuss the question. After about 4 minutes have everyone return their attention to you, and invite two or three people to share what was discussed in their small group with the larger group.

Some stories help us make sense of life. Today we're going to look at a few of the stories—also called parables—Jesus told to help others understand the kingdom of God. Parables share more than facts and figures. They communicate important truths in a dynamic and interesting way. And the parables that Jesus told often used a common object or situation to help people understand more about God or God's kingdom. To help us get a better grasp on this, I'd like us to try something. I'll start.

Show everyone the item you brought and tell why this is meaningful and what it helps others understand about you.

Now I'd like you to find an item that you have with you or think of an item from home. Show that item or tell about it, and share the short story of this item and how it can help others know something new about you.

Let the groups tell their stories based on items they have with them or can

LEADER GUIDE

LESSON 6: WHY DID JESUS TELL SUCH CONFUSING STORIES?   53

tell about. Allow 4 or 5 minutes for sharing, and then call everyone's attention back to you.

Did you learn something new about someone in your group? And the next time you see an item like one described by someone in your group, will you think of that person? Stories like these can help us have a different level of understanding. And with that in mind, we're looking at a selection of Matthew that has several of the parables Jesus used to tell about what the kingdom of God is like.

GROUNDING

Let's get grounded in God's Word. Today's Bible account is from Matthew 13:24-45. Before we start, here are a few interesting facts: Matthew is the only Gospel to describe the nature and makeup of the church (*ekklesia*, from which we get the word "ecclesial"), and Matthew is also the only Gospel to use the word "church." It also has more of Jesus' teaching than Mark, Luke, or John. Now, let's dig in.

Read Matthew 13:24-45 aloud, or ask for a volunteer from your group to read it aloud. Today's Scripture is on the long side, so you might want to divide it up for two or three volunteer readers. Encourage everyone else to follow along in their own Bibles or in their participant guides.

God's Word: Matthew 13:24-45

24 Jesus told them another parable: "The kingdom of heaven is like a man who sowed good seed in his field. 25 But while everyone was sleeping, his enemy came and sowed weeds among the wheat, and went away. 26 When the wheat sprouted and formed heads, then the weeds also appeared.

27 "The owner's servants came to him and said, 'Sir, didn't you sow good seed in your field? Where then did the weeds come from?'

28 "'An enemy did this,' he replied.

"The servants asked him, 'Do you want us to go and pull them up?'

29 "'No,' he answered, 'because while you are pulling the weeds, you may uproot the wheat with them. 30 Let both grow together until the harvest. At that time I will tell the harvesters: First collect the weeds and tie them in bundles to be

FEARLESS CONVERSATION: **WHY IS JESUS SO RADICAL?**

burned; then gather the wheat and bring it into my barn.'"

³¹ He told them another parable: "The kingdom of heaven is like a mustard seed, which a man took and planted in his field. ³² Though it is the smallest of all seeds, yet when it grows, it is the largest of garden plants and becomes a tree, so that the birds come and perch in its branches."

³³ He told them still another parable: "The kingdom of heaven is like yeast that a woman took and mixed into about sixty pounds of flour until it worked all through the dough."

³⁴ Jesus spoke all these things to the crowd in parables; he did not say anything to them without using a parable. ³⁵ So was fulfilled what was spoken through the prophet:

"I will open my mouth in parables,

I will utter things hidden since the creation of the world."

³⁶ Then he left the crowd and went into the house. His disciples came to him and said, "Explain to us the parable of the weeds in the field."

³⁷ He answered, "The one who sowed the good seed is the Son of Man. ³⁸ The field is the world, and the good seed stands for the people of the kingdom. The weeds are the people of the evil one, ³⁹ and the enemy who sows them is the devil. The harvest is the end of the age, and the harvesters are angels.

⁴⁰ "As the weeds are pulled up and burned in the fire, so it will be at the end of the age. ⁴¹ The Son of Man will send out his angels, and they will weed out of his kingdom everything that causes sin and all who do evil. ⁴² They will throw them into the blazing furnace, where there will be weeping and gnashing of teeth. ⁴³ Then the righteous will shine like the sun in the kingdom of their Father. Whoever has ears, let them hear."

⁴⁴ "The kingdom of heaven is like treasure hidden in a field. When a man found it, he hid it again, and then in his joy went and sold all he had and bought that field. ⁴⁵ "Again, the kingdom of heaven is like a merchant looking for fine pearls."

Before we discuss this I'd like you to take a moment to reflect.

- **Does anything strike you as unusual or interesting about these parables?**

Would they hold the attention of a modern audience (why or why not)?

Capture your initial thoughts and questions in your participant guide.

LESSON 6: WHY DID JESUS TELL SUCH CONFUSING STORIES?

Leader Guide

Wait at least 1 minute—or even a little longer—so people can jot down their questions or thoughts before moving forward. This should be something people do on their own rather than in discussion groups. When it appears that everyone is ready to move on, continue.

GRAPPLING

We'll get to your questions and thoughts in a bit. But let's grapple with a few other questions first. The thing about a topic like this is the fact that we all have an opinion and a different point of view. And all of them are welcome here. So let's make an extra effort to respect each other and listen to others before we jump in with our own thoughts. Let's respect the opinions of others in the same way we want ours respected. And above all, let's trust God to guide our conversation and lead us to truth.

Pray for the group to be open to hearing each other and to hearing God. Ask God to open hearts to be receptive to each other, and ask God to direct the conversation where it needs to go.

LEADER LEARNING

Encourage everyone to be part of the conversation, whether in their small group or as they share with the larger group. Listening shows respect for a person, even if you don't agree with that person's opinion.

BEHIND THE SCENES

In this passage, Jesus describes a kingdom that is in the present and in the future. The Kingdom is here, but it is not entirely here yet. We are confronted by the reality of the Kingdom in the present. But we will only experience God's kingdom fully when it comes in the future. Notice that Jesus says, "The kingdom is at hand."

The parables were designed to show this present/future connection. Each parable is a multi-layered story. In the parable of the weeds, the weeds are a problem now but their ultimate solution can only come about through future actions.

This section also shows us something about Jesus himself and the importance of his message. Even though Jesus knew that many people would not receive him and many would reject him, he shared his message and his life with them and continued to minister to them with compassion.

Let's talk about this passage. Look on page 46 of your participant guide and refer to the first question under the "Grappling" heading. Talk about this for about 5 minutes in your small group, and then we'll

hear some reports back to the larger group.

• **Though Jesus was talking directly to the people with him, he's also talking to us through these parables. What message do you find in the parables we've read?**

Allow about 5 minutes for discussion, and then have each group share something they feel is significant. Thank everyone for sharing.

BEHIND THE SCENES

In the parable of the mustard seed, Jesus used one of the smallest seeds known to his audience to illustrate a very big point. The plant that grows from the tiny mustard seed can grow to be between 8 to 10 feet tall around the Lake of Galilee. This fact vividly illustrated Jesus' point that the small can become mighty.

Jesus used illustrations from everyday life to make his point. In what other ways were the parables meant to be effective?

Let's talk about this next question as a large group.

• **Based on these parables, what do you think the kingdom of heaven is like?**

Allow time for different people to share their thoughts with the whole group. Remember to model and encourage listening and respect for others as they share. When several people have had a chance to respond, continue.

There's a lot to consider in this section of Matthew! Jesus speaks in parables that spoke on some level to his audience—but confused many of them as well. This section of the Bible is sure to have raised questions in your own mind. Let's take time now to grapple with the questions or thoughts you wrote down after we read the Scripture. Take time to share those with your small group as you are comfortable, and talk together about these ideas and questions.

Allow at least 10 minutes for groups to talk. Give a 1-minute warning so groups have time to finish their thoughts.

What did you talk about? Let's hear ideas or questions that your group found interesting.

Allow a few minutes for different groups to share. Depending on how much time you have left you can simply let groups report their insights and questions, or if you have time you can invite the larger group to

LESSON 6: WHY DID JESUS TELL SUCH CONFUSING STORIES?

Leader Guide

respond to an insight or question that was shared.

BEHIND THE SCENES

While the parables were meant to reveal hidden principles and truths, there was also hidden truth in the actions of Christ himself. Matthew's Gospel depicts Jesus as the Messiah, and the scenes Matthew favors are those that symbolically portray Jesus as a king interacting with his subjects. Not an aloof, power-wielding king showing off for the people, but a benevolent ruler making himself known and forming relationships with the ones he came to bring the kingdom of heaven to.

LEADER LEARNING

Remember, *I don't know* and *I'm not sure* are acceptable answers. Sometimes we don't know something or we need more time to let things "marinate" and be examined in a quiet place between just God and the individual. Not every question will have a simple answer (in fact, most won't), but this is a chance to invite people to participate in the process of exploration. Encourage people to keep digging into those hard questions long after your Sunday school class is over.

In this passage, Jesus is speaking to those in his hometown, to those who we would think would be the most loyal to him. But they turned out to be the ones who had little faith in Jesus. And it's clear that many of the people who heard these parables didn't understand them. Could it be that they didn't understand them because they didn't accept Jesus or his message? They clearly did not believe he was God's Son, so they would not spend much time trying to "decipher" the meaning of the parables.

Chapter 13 of Matthew closes with the words, "And he did not do many miracles there because of their lack of faith." Jesus' profound teachings didn't persuade the people of his own hometown.

How might our belief or lack of belief in Jesus affect our understanding of his message? Can someone who does not believe that Jesus is God's Son still understand the message of the Bible? What do you think? Let's talk about this as a large group.

- **Can someone who does not believe that Jesus is God's Son still understand the message of the Bible?**

Invite people to share their thoughts with the rest of the group. Be sure to thank people for being fearless in their conversation.

FEARLESS CONVERSATION: **WHY IS JESUS SO RADICAL?**

GROWING

In this account in Matthew, we begin to see a shift in Jesus' focus. He is placing more responsibility on the disciples and is preparing them for the days to come when they will be the ones who bear the responsibility of carrying his message.

Matthew 13:24-45 gives us an insight into two major biblical themes: the kingdom of heaven/God and Jesus' place in that kingdom. It emphasizes the nearness of the kingdom and the fact that the full realization of the kingdom is still "in the future." It is like a great celebration that has been planned and arranged, and the potential guests have been issued invitations and are waiting for the big day.

And even though the event has been planned and the date set (we just don't know when the date is), God is still active through his Son, Jesus, making sure every invitation has been delivered and every guest has had a chance to respond.

Let's consider our personal responses to Jesus. There are two last questions in this lesson in your participant guide. Take time now to reflect on these and journal your thoughts and reflections.

- How were the people of Galilee who heard these parables like or unlike us today? More specifically, how do you see yourself in them?

- As we move through this quarter, we'll continually be exploring the question, Why is Jesus so radical? Based only on what we've discussed today, what's one sentence that might answer that question?

Allow time for people to adequately reflect and journal; then close with a prayer, thanking God that we can approach him and each other without fear.

LESSON 6: WHY DID JESUS TELL SUCH CONFUSING STORIES?

FEARLESS CONVERSATION

WHY IS JESUS SO RADICAL?

LESSON 7: WAS JESUS RACIST, OR SEXIST—OR BOTH?

LEADER PREP

- Read the entire lesson ahead of time. Also read the corresponding pages in the Why Is Jesus So Radical? Participant Guide as there may be additional material provided there that will be helpful to you.

- You'll find "Behind the Scenes" boxes with Bible commentary provided throughout this lesson. They're there to help you gain a better understanding of the Bible. The people in your group will have these too.

- Pray. Lots.

GREETING

- Welcome everyone and be sure to introduce yourself.

- Be sure everyone has a copy of the participant guide.

- Let everyone know you'll be moving through Lesson 7 today, so they can find that section in the guide and use this to guide them through today's lesson.

- Explain that there are many "Behind the Scenes" commentary notes throughout the lesson. These can be read by participants as they come to that section of the lesson—or people who want to plan ahead can read

Leader Guide

them during the week to be ready for the next lesson.

Then ask:

Tell me something about faith. What exactly is it? It's a pretty amazing concept, so don't worry that it's hard to describe. Give it a shot!

Let people share their definitions of faith with the larger group, then say:

Let's get into smaller groups and talk a little more about this thing called faith. First, go ahead and get into a small group of no more than four people and introduce yourselves.

Allow a minute for people to do this, then continue.

I want you think about two people: God and the person you feel closest to. It can be a spouse, a friend, a parent. That's up to you. Without discussing this with those in your group, finish the two sentences you see there in your participant book as they relate to these people. One relates to your faith in the person you are closest to, and the other relates to your faith in God. I'll give you 1 minute to do that.

Let people complete the two sentences in their books without discussing these yet.

When it appears that everyone has completed this, have small groups talk about what they wrote and answer the question that follows those sentences.

- **Why do you think faith is important in a relationship—whether with God or with a person?**

Allow about 5 minutes for sharing and discussion, and then have groups turn their attention back to you.

Thank you for sharing. As we look at these ideas we start to realize that faith goes beyond knowing something. Faith is knowing something that may not have tangible proof. It is knowing something in your heart and not just your head. And with that in mind, let's dig into a rather bizarre confrontation between Jesus and a Canaanite woman.

GROUNDING

Let's get grounded in God's Word so we can understand more about the radical approach Jesus took in connecting with people. Today's Bible account is from Matthew 15:21-28. Matthew has related an incident that on the surface raises some odd questions about Jesus. Is he a racist? Is he sexist? Has he lost sight of why he came to earth in the first place? Let's read the account and see if we can make sense of this encounter.

Read Matthew 15:21-28 aloud, or ask a volunteer from your group to read it aloud. Encourage everyone else to follow along in their own Bibles or in their participant guides.

God's Word: Matthew 15:21-28

21 Leaving that place, Jesus withdrew to the region of Tyre and Sidon. 22 A Canaanite woman from that vicinity came to him, crying out, "Lord, Son of David, have mercy on me! My daughter is demon-possessed and suffering terribly."

23 Jesus did not answer a word. So his disciples came to him and urged him, "Send her away, for she keeps crying out after us."

24 He answered, "I was sent only to the lost sheep of Israel."

25 The woman came and knelt before him. "Lord, help me!" she said.

26 He replied, "It is not right to take the children's bread and toss it to the dogs."

27 "Yes it is, Lord," she said. "Even the dogs eat the crumbs that fall from their master's table."

28 Then Jesus said to her, "Woman, you have great faith! Your request is granted." And her daughter was healed at that moment.

Before we discuss this, take a moment to reflect.

- **What jumps out at you and catches your attention in this passage? What questions do you have?**

Leader Guide

Capture those initial thoughts and questions in your participant guide.

Wait at least 1 minute so people can jot down their questions or thoughts before moving forward. This should be something that people do on their own—not in discussion groups. When it appears that everyone is ready to move on, continue.

GRAPPLING

We'll return to those questions you wrote down in a bit—so thanks for capturing them now so you won't forget them! As we move into this discussion, let's remember to be respectful to each other by listening and being open in our sharing. Above all, let's trust that God is here and is guiding this conversation. I'd like to invite God to be part of our discussion right now.

Pray for the group to be open to hearing each other and to hearing God. Ask God to open hearts to be receptive to each other, and ask God to direct the conversation in the direction it needs to go.

LEADER LEARNING

This account seems so unlike Jesus. But as we explore further, the real significance of this passage will become more apparent. So roll up your sleeves and dig in. God may be directing the conversation to an area that will have even greater impact on the lives of those in your group than you could imagine.

BEHIND THE SCENES

Matthew 15:21-28 can be a little hard to hear if we take it at face value. On the surface, a woman approaches Jesus and he makes her all but beg for her daughter's healing. But on closer inspection we see this as another turning point in Jesus' ministry. In verse 24 he says, "I was sent only to the lost sheep of Israel." And in this instance he was talking about Israel in general. As it says in Isaiah 53:6, "We all, like sheep, have gone astray, each of us has turned to our own way; and the Lord has laid on him the iniquity of us all." Jesus' mission was originally to reveal himself as the Messiah they were expecting.

But there was something in the persistent faith of the Canaanite woman that touched Jesus. She humbles herself to the point of saying even the dogs get scraps from their masters' tables, and Jesus cannot refuse her. She has recognized him as the Messiah and approached him with faith and reverence.

At first glance, this Jesus doesn't seem much like the Sunday school Jesus: the gentle man who's nice

to children, always has time for people, and gets angry only when someone's abusing the Temple or cheating people. In this encounter we see a Jesus who appears to be having a very bad day. What's your response to the Jesus we meet in this passage…and why?

You'll talk about this for about 5 minutes in your small group, and then we'll hear some reports back to the larger group.

- **What's your response to the Jesus we meet in this passage, and why?**

Allow 5 minutes for discussion, and then have each group share something they feel is significant. Thank everyone for sharing.

Let's talk about this next question as a larger group. Here is a woman literally begging Jesus for help. And at first he refuses. Some people think Jesus was testing the woman to see how strong her faith was.

- **Why would Jesus need to test anyone's faith? And in what ways do you think Jesus tests our faith today, if ever?**

Allow time for different people to share their thoughts with the whole group.

Remember to model and encourage listening and respect for others as they share. When several people have had a chance to respond, continue.

BEHIND THE SCENES

Was Jesus racist? As we come into the scene, Jesus has taken some time to rest. But the place he has stopped to recharge is in the land of the Canaanites. They were in many ways the biblical enemies of Israel because their paganism had often led Israel into idolatry. If Jesus was a racist, it seems unlikely that he would choose to stop and relax in a place where there was animosity.

It's possible that he went to the region of Tyre and Sidon because that is the last place people would expect a Jew to go. Or what other reasons might Jesus have had for choosing this location as a rest stop?

I'd like us to have a chance to share in our groups about our own observations and questions. Take time now to share anything that seemed especially relevant to you as we read from Matthew 15, as well as the questions that popped into your mind. Your group can discuss those questions if you're willing to tackle them!

Allow at least 10 minutes for groups to talk. Give a 1-minute alert so groups have time to finish their thoughts.

LEADER GUIDE

LESSON 7: WAS JESUS RACIST, OR SEXIST—OR BOTH?

Leader Guide

Let's hear what was discussed. Is anyone willing to share a bit about the conversation from your group?

Allow a few minutes for groups to share. Depending on how much time you have left you can simply let groups report their insights and questions, or if you have time you can invite the larger group to respond to an insight or question that was shared.

LEADER LEARNING

Remember that no answer is insignificant. Avoid brushing off the thoughts of others or thinking they are not relevant. Treat every person with respect. It takes courage to share openly in Sunday school!

BEHIND THE SCENES

Was Jesus sexist? Let's face it: He called the woman a dog. Or did he?

In this instance Jesus is referring to Jews as children and to Gentiles as dogs. Not the wild, feral dogs that roamed the land, but the mild-mannered house dogs. Jesus used this comparison to allude to his mission and show the Jews he was the Messiah. Jesus made a similar reference in Mark 7:27, "'First let the children eat all they want,' he told her, 'for it is not right to take the children's bread and toss it to the dogs.'" And the Canaanite woman, who called Jesus "Lord" through the whole exchange, was not offended by the reference because she understood who Jesus was. And she also understood that he was her daughter's only hope.

The faith he was hoping to instill in the Jews was vital and alive in this Gentile woman. And because of her faith, his mission enlarged to include the Gentiles. In other words, she was the mom who changed the world.

GROWING

This account is one of those that, on first reading, can be a shocker. But as we peel away the layers of culture and the norms of the day, we can see the true meaning of the encounter.

The account related in Matthew 15:21-28 contains a first. This woman's daughter was not the first Gentile who Jesus healed. But her daughter was the first Gentile healed outside the Jewish territory. It was the first time Jesus ever healed a Gentile in their own land. Similar to the woman at the well referred to in the book of John, (John 4:25-29), this Canaanite woman publicly acknowledged Jesus as the Messiah ("Lord, son of David, have mercy on me!") even before the disciples had done so.

This woman believed Jesus was

the Messiah, and her faith forced her to persevere in pursuing Jesus. Have you ever had the same level of perseverance? Let's talk about this in our small groups—and I'd like you to also pray together, especially for anyone who shares about being in a time of persevering right now.

- **Tell about a time you persevered in your faith, or perhaps you are in a situation like this right now that you're willing to share about.**

Allow at least 8 minutes for groups to share and pray. Then continue.

The conclusion of this meeting between Jesus and the Canaanite woman is more than Jesus relenting and healing her daughter. It is the apex of a story about grace; about strong faith; and about the Kingdom, which will come to the Jews, the Gentiles, and ultimately all the world. Jesus is making it clear that, despite the fact he was sent to the Jews as the Messiah, his grace and his mercy are for the entire world. No exceptions.

Let's reflect on what this means to us personally.

Direct people to the last section for this lesson in the participant guide. There are two questions for personal reflection there. Allow time for participants to read and reflect, and then close the time with a brief prayer.

LEADER GUIDE

LESSON 7: WAS JESUS RACIST, OR SEXIST—OR BOTH?

FEARLESS CONVERSATION™

WHY IS JESUS SO RADICAL?

LESSON 8: WHAT'S JESUS GOT AGAINST GROWN-UPS?

LEADER PREP

- Read the entire lesson ahead of time. Also read the corresponding pages in the Why Is Jesus So Radical? Participant Guide as there may be additional material provided there that will be helpful for your preparation.

- Read the "Behind the Scenes" boxes. If you're in a hurry, it would be tempting to skip these. However, they are loaded with biblical commentary that will help you better understand the lesson you are about to teach. The people in your group will have these as well.

- Spend time in prayer asking God to help you facilitate the discussion. Ask God to prepare the hearts of your participants as well.

GREETING

- Welcome everyone and be sure to introduce yourself.

- Be sure everyone has a copy of the participant guide.

- Let everyone know you'll be moving through Lesson 8 today, so they can find that section in their guide and use it to prompt them through today's lesson.

- Remind people about the "Behind the Scenes" commentary notes throughout the lesson. They can be used as helps during discussion groups or for advanced preparation to prepare for the lesson.

Leader Guide

As a way to get to know each other a bit better, let's take a poll to see how long it's been since you've done any babysitting. Take a second and try to remember the last time you watched a child who wasn't your own.

Let's start with who's watched a child most recently. Did anyone watch or take care of a child who was not your own yesterday?

Encourage people to raise their hands if they babysat a child yesterday. If nobody has, keep going back a day or even a week at a time until you identify a participant as the group's most recent babysitter. Have everyone else give that person a round of applause.

Now let's find out who has had the longest break from watching someone else's child. Let's start with one year. If you haven't watched someone else's child in the past year, stand up.

Allow people to stand.

If you haven't watched someone else's child in the past 18 months remain standing. Everyone else may have a seat.

Continue adding two or three months and repeat the exercise until you identify the person who has gone the longest without babysitting. Don't be surprised if you end up with a handful of people who simply can't remember how long it's been!

Fantastic. Now you all know who you might trust with your children and who needs a refresher course before you drop your darlings off. Let's talk more about this topic in smaller groups.

Have people get into groups of about four and introduce themselves. When this is done, continue.

In your groups, talk about how you feel when you're asked to watch a child for a few hours.

- **Are you usually happy to babysit, or does it feel like an imposition? Share why you answer as you do.**

Give the groups about 5 minutes to answer. When you sense the conversation is winding down, gather everyone's attention and have someone from each group share their findings with everyone.

Let's talk a bit more in our small groups. We just looked at some of

FEARLESS CONVERSATION: **WHY IS JESUS SO RADICAL?**

our own attitudes toward children; now let's look at our culture's attitudes toward children. With your group, consider the next three questions in your participant guide. You'll only have about 5 minutes to discuss these—so the point is not to dig deeply into each question, but to share some quick insights based on these three questions.

- If all you had to judge society's attitude toward children was a copy of the TV Guide, what conclusions might you come up with?

- If you visited a nice restaurant and had to make conclusions about the role of children in society based on what you saw, what opinions might you form?

- If a stranger visited our church and walked around, what would he or she say about how we valued children?

Allow the groups about 5 minutes to discuss the questions found in their participant guides. At the end of the time, ask someone from each group to summarize their findings.

Our culture seems to have conflicting opinions about children. We invest so much money in their safety, education, and entertainment. But on the other hand, children are often viewed as burdens that get in the way of our own pursuit of happiness. We're going to discover that Jesus' view of children was radically different than that of his culture. But I'm getting ahead of myself!

BEHIND THE SCENES

Jesus was a master at radically turning over "sacred conventions" and assumptions, offering a new way to relate to God and others. Children in the Old Testament were valued and a sign of blessing for their parents, who gained honor and prestige as their family grew. There was nothing wrong with that, but Jesus "flipped" that idea by saying that the honor of children is not in what they provide for parents but in how they approach God in total humility. In a similar way, Jesus "flips" the idea of patriarchal honor and privilege in the parable of the prodigal son (Luke 15:11-32). One scholar says the title should be the "Parable of the Crazy Father," since the father does everything "wrong" according to long-held customs in regard to both his sons. Yet Jesus clearly indicates that God is like the crazy father in the parable.

What other things did Jesus "flip" in his ministry?

LEADER GUIDE

GROUNDING

Let's ground ourselves in God's Word so we can better understand what Jesus meant when he said we need to become like little children to enter the kingdom of heaven. Today's Bible account is from Luke 18:15-17. It's interesting that Luke sandwiched this short account between a long section of parables. It's as if he believed this true-to-life event had the capacity to teach in a way that was similar to how Jesus' parables worked.

Read Luke 18:15-17 aloud, or invite a volunteer to read it aloud. Encourage everyone else to follow along in their Bibles or in their participant guides.

Before we discuss this I'd like you to take a moment to reflect.

- **When you read this passage, what jumps out at you and grabs your attention?**

Record your thoughts and questions in your participant guide.

Allow people a minute or two to record their thoughts and questions before continuing with the lesson. Tell them that this is an exercise they should be doing on their own—not in discussion groups. Once everyone appears to be finished and ready to proceed, continue.

BEHIND THE SCENES

The image of becoming a child seemed to be Jesus' metaphor of choice when attempting to convince those in the religious establishment that their system of good works and adherence to their strict interpretation of the law of Moses did nothing to make them worthy of being citizens of God's kingdom. In John 3, Nicodemus, a Pharisee, makes a midnight visit to Jesus to secretly inquire how to become right with God. Nicodemus wasn't an average Pharisee. John describes him as "Israel's teacher." He knew the Mosaic law inside and out and had the reputation of being a prominent authority on the ▶

God's Word: Luke 18:15-17

¹⁵ People were also bringing babies to Jesus for him to place his hands on them. When the disciples saw this, they rebuked them. ¹⁶ But Jesus called the children to him and said, "Let the little children come to me, and do not hinder them, for the kingdom of God belongs to such as these. ¹⁷ Truly I tell you, anyone who will not receive the kingdom of God like a little child will never enter it."

topic. Jesus responded to him by telling him he needed to be reborn from above. Nicodemus was perfectly powerless, despite his impressive religious pedigree. Many theologians believe Nicodemus placed his faith in God, although in secret due to his position, since he reappears at the end of John's Gospel to assist with Jesus' burial.

Pray for the group to be open to hearing each other and hearing God. Ask God to open hearts and to be receptive to each other—and ask God to steer the conversation wherever he wants it to go.

GRAPPLING

You've all compiled a list of impressions and questions, and we'll come back to that in a bit. But first we're going to grapple with a few other questions. Let's be mindful to create a safe environment for sharing. We'll all be respectful of each other's opinions, even if we don't see eye to eye. We'll listen before we jump in with our own perspectives. We believe that God is in this conversation and brought each one of us here. This means that our differing opinions have the ability to bring us to a greater understanding of what God is telling us in the passage. So let's invite God into our conversation right now.

BEHIND THE SCENES

This week's account is short—only three verses long—but it's enough to reveal Jesus' inclusiveness when it comes to who can participate in his kingdom. Some scholars believe the concept of childhood wasn't as fully formed in Bible times as it is today. Children were marginalized until they were old enough to contribute to the greater good. The text in the original language reveals that the parents were bringing infants and toddlers to Jesus, so these were the least valuable of people, according to the culture at the time. Mothers didn't bond with their children as strongly as mothers and children bond today due to the high infant and child mortality rates. The Romans—Israel's oppressors—routinely exposed unwanted children to the elements. This practice was prohibited, but it's clear from this passage that children didn't enjoy the same social status as adults. An onlooker could have seen Jesus' behavior and decided that if he had time for children, then he had time for anyone.

But Jesus goes a step further and lifts children up as an example of what someone needs to be like in order to enter God's kingdom. He doesn't specify how we need to be like children, but instead leaves it for his disciples to struggle with.

LEADER GUIDE

LESSON 8: WHAT'S JESUS GOT AGAINST GROWN-UPS? **73**

Leader Guide

Children weren't valued as much in ancient cultures as they are in our culture today. But clearly their parents still cared enough about them to bring them to Jesus. But they were turned away by the disciples—and then Jesus, in turn, held up children as a positive role model for what it means to able to receive the kingdom of heaven. There are two questions in your participant guide related to this. Talk about these in your small groups, and then we'll hear reports back to the larger group.

- **Why do you think the disciples scolded the parents of the children? What could be their reasoning for this?**

- **Why do you think Jesus held up children as a positive role model for what it means to be able to receive the kingdom of heaven?**

Allow the groups to discuss for 8 to 10 minutes. Have someone from each group offer their groups' suggestions. Thank everyone for sharing.

I want to give us all a chance to share in our groups about our own observations and questions. Now is the time to share anything that seemed especially meaningful to you as we read from Luke 18. And if you're comfortable, toss out any of the questions the passage raised for you. Perhaps someone else has an insight that will shed some light on the topic.

LEADER LEARNING

As you lead your group to understand that God wants them to relate to him as children and trust him to be their good Father, keep in mind that some people in your group may not have had good examples of fathers in their homes growing up. Some experienced absent fathers, others had fathers who worked so much to provide that they were emotionally unavailable, while others simply had fathers with poor parenting skills. So while some in your group will immediately resonate with Jesus' teaching, others will find themselves struggling to connect with his words. Don't feel pressure to fix this situation. Allow people to be where they are. If someone is brave and discloses the source of their discomfort, affirm their commitment to being vulnerable and contributing to the fearless conversation. Express your confidence that, over time, God will reveal himself as his or her trustworthy Father.

Allow at least 10 minutes for groups to talk. Give a 1-minute "let's wrap it up!" warning so groups have time to finish their thoughts. You can use the remaining time to allow people from each group to report back their insights and questions. If you feel pinched for time, consider focusing on "burning question" that a group was unable to answer. Just remember that you aren't responsible to have the final answer. It's healthy to admit what you don't know and ask the larger group if anyone is interested in researching the answer during the week.

Jesus made a point of welcoming one the most unvalued people groups that anyone could imagine in his culture. By doing so, he made it clear that no one was unimportant to him and that he was given access to the kingdom of God. But he went a step further and pointed out how these children had qualities that needed to be imitated by anyone who hoped to have his or her relationship with God restored. If Jesus walked the earth in our times, what people group do you think he would use to communicate the same truths? Why?

Invite people to share their thoughts with the rest of the group. As always, thank people for being willing to contribute to this fearless conversation.

BEHIND THE SCENES

Sandwich-ing: Sometimes Luke intentionally puts one passage in the middle of two others to make a point. Our account is "sandwiched" between a parable and the account of a rich ruler who wanted to know how to enter the kingdom of heaven. This sandwiching of accounts lets us see three different responses to Jesus and consider which response Jesus honors most. If you want greater context for today's reading, dig into this entire chapter in Luke for more!

GROWING

We're going to close this session with some personal reflection. In your participant guides, look for these questions and reflect on them there.

- **How do you view your relationship with Jesus? In what ways do you approach Jesus as a trusting child, and in what ways do you remind yourself of the scolding disciples?**

- **What is one step (even a "baby" step) you could take to relate more deeply as a child of God?**

Invite everyone to write their reflections in the space provided in their participant guides as well as

LEADER GUIDE

the theme question on what makes Jesus radical. Allow time for people to adequately reflect and journal, then close with a prayer, thanking God for being a good and loving parent who we can trust. Pray for faith to totally trust in God just as infants totally trust their parents.

FEARLESS CONVERSATION

WHY IS JESUS SO RADICAL?

LESSON 9: WHAT WAS REALLY GOING ON AT JESUS' "TRIUMPHAL ENTRY" INTO JERUSALEM?

LEADER PREP

- Read the entire lesson ahead of time. Also read the corresponding pages in the Why Is Jesus So Radical? Participant Guide as there may be additional material provided there that will be helpful for your preparation.

- Read the "Behind the Scenes" boxes. If you're in a hurry, it would be tempting to skip these. However, they're loaded with biblical commentary that will help you better understand the lesson you are about to lead. The people in your group will have these as well.

- Pray. Lots.

FOR EXTRA IMPACT

Collect several magazines that feature recognizable celebrities, sports figures, and politicians. If you aren't able to do so, it's okay—but your group will have more fun if you're able to collect them.

Prep Notes:

_____

_____

LEADER GUIDE

GREETING

- Welcome everyone and introduce yourself.

- Be sure everyone has a copy of the participant guide.

- Let everyone know you'll be working through Lesson 9 today, so they can find that section in the guide and use this to prompt them through today's lesson.

- Remind them to use the "Behind the Scenes" sections to find important insights about today's passage to help them better engage with Scripture.

Then ask:

Have you been around a person who everyone seemed to either like a lot or dislike a lot? Maybe you've encountered that person at a party or at work—or even at your family Christmas party! Without sharing names, what is it about the person you're thinking of that causes people to have such as strong reaction, either good or bad?

Allow several people to respond. When the sharing begins to taper off, continue.

Let's get into small groups and talk about this a little more. Get into groups of four, and make a list of the most polarizing celebrities and public figures you can think of. And when I say polarizing, I'm not talking about the bears that live in the Arctic.☺ Think of people on both ends—"strongly like" and "strongly dislike"—of the scale. And you may have some disagreement in your group—you might really like someone who another person in your group strongly dislikes! That's okay!

If you brought magazines in, give each group a few, which they can use for reference as they are brainstorming public figures. These are not essential to the discussion, but may help people think of people who fit both categories more quickly. (If you didn't bring magazines, just ask your group to brainstorm the most polarizing people they can think of.)

Allow 4 minutes for people to get into small groups, introduce themselves, and brainstorm the most polarizing public figures they can think of or find in their magazines. After about 4 minutes, have someone from each group share their most polarizing person from each end of the scale and what it is about that public figure that garnishes such positive or negative reactions from people.

LEADER LEARNING

In our culture of contentious politics, it's highly likely that one of the names listed will be that of a nationally recognized political figure. Acknowledge the fact that most people have a strong opinion regarding this person, but don't share your personal political views. Share that you love the fact that your church is able to attract Christians from diverse political backgrounds and that you need to move on to avoid a lengthy tangent that will distract from the lesson. This is a good practice to adopt whenever an off-topic, hot-button subject comes up. If the contentious topic is relevant to the lesson, by all means jump into a fearless conversation— otherwise, avoid letting your lesson become derailed.

So these names that have been shared are our finalists for most polarizing person. The fact that they are polarizing is not only based on opinions about whether these people are right or wrong. We're basing this on the person who gets the strongest and most diverse reactions from others.

Here's a question for you to take back to your small groups.

Imagine you found yourself being a polarizing person, maybe based on your personality, a leadership position you hold, or a cause you are passionate about.

- **What would it be like to be that polarizing person? How would you deal with the pressure of being under so much scrutiny?**

Allow groups 4 minutes to discuss the question. When you sense the conversation is slowing down, gather everyone's attention back to you. Allow for volunteers to share what their groups discussed.

Before we move on into our Bible story, let's explore one more potentially polarizing figure.

- **On a scale of 1 to 10, how polarizing is Jesus in our culture? Why?**

Allow several people to share their opinions with the larger group. Once everyone has had a chance to share their perspective, continue.

In today's Bible account, we see Jesus take a bold and polarizing move that forced everyone around him to take a firm stand over who they believed Jesus to be. It was an uncharacteristic move for Jesus,

Leader Guide

but it marked a shift in the focus of his ministry. Let's press on to discover what that move was and why he did it.

BEHIND THE SCENES

In Luke, Jesus resisted allowing others to publically identify him up to this point. After healing someone, he would often send that person off with strict instructions to tell no one. Jesus possessed a keen awareness that "his time had not yet come." But now, he chooses to enter Jerusalem in a choreographed manner that seems to encourage a response from the crowds. Now he allows the crowds to publically adore him as the Christ. He is forcing everyone to have an opinion about him. He chose to enter Jerusalem when it was teaming with Jewish pilgrims, who were returning from all over the known world to celebrate the Passover. Historians note that Jerusalem's streets were barely passable. This was the moment for his grand entrance.

The Old Testament prophet Zechariah predicted that Israel's Messiah and rightful King would enter the Holy City with gentleness and humility, riding on a donkey (Zechariah 9:9). This modest entrance would stand out, as it was customary for conquering rulers of the day to enter a newly defeated city on a proud war horse. Jesus carefully fulfilled the prophecy in a way that both symbolically fulfilled the prophecy and signaled the nature of his kingship.

Although this passage is commonly referred to as "The Triumphal Entry," Luke doesn't continue the narrative long enough for Jesus to enter the city. He was on the move, riding and forcing everyone around him to make a choice about who he is.

The crowds who had followed his teaching and healing ministry turned out to greet Jesus on the way and publically adore him as their King. The crowds openly received Jesus as their rightful ruler. They were so convinced Jesus was the Chosen One, who would use military force to drive out their oppressors, they were unbothered by the fact that armed Roman soldiers were stationed inside Jerusalem's walls.

The Pharisees, however, were quite bothered by the public demonstration. They approached Jesus and demanded he silence his followers, presumably to keep them from calling down the wrath of their Roman oppressors. But Jesus is very clear: The time had arrived for Jerusalem to recognize their rightful King. Stones would declare the truth if necessary.

GROUNDING

Let's get grounded in God's Word so we can begin to understand just how provocative Jesus was being with his actions. Today's Bible account is from Luke 19:28-40. Luke, the author of the book, would have been keenly aware of just how politically volatile Jesus' triumphal entry was. Israel was occupied by the Romans, and the Jews were not completely free to practice their religion without interference. Let's read the passage to see how Jesus' actions risked provoking the wrath of the greatest superpower on earth.

Read Luke 19:28-40 aloud, or invite a volunteer to read it aloud. Encourage everyone else to follow along in their own Bibles or in their participant guides.

God's Word: Luke 19:28-40

28 After telling this story, Jesus went on toward Jerusalem, walking ahead of his disciples. 29 As he came to the towns of Bethphage and Bethany on the Mount of Olives, he sent two disciples ahead. 30 "Go into that village over there," he told them. "As you enter it, you will see a young donkey tied there that no one has ever ridden. Untie it and bring it here. 31 If anyone asks, 'Why are you untying that colt?' just say, 'The Lord needs it.'"

32 So they went and found the colt, just as Jesus had said. 33 And sure enough, as they were untying it, the owners asked them, "Why are you untying that colt?"

34 And the disciples simply replied, "The Lord needs it." 35 So they brought the colt to Jesus and threw their garments over it for him to ride on.

36 As he rode along, the crowds spread out their garments on the road ahead of him. 37 When he reached the place where the road started down the Mount of Olives, all of his followers began to shout and sing as they walked along, praising God for all the wonderful miracles they had seen.

38 "Blessings on the King who comes in the name of the Lord! Peace in heaven, and glory in highest heaven!"

39 But some of the Pharisees among the crowd said, "Teacher, rebuke your followers for saying things like that!"

40 He replied, "If they kept quiet, the stones along the road would burst into cheers!"

Before we discuss this, I'd like you to take a moment to capture your first impressions of this passage.

- **What questions immediately come to mind? What gets your attention?**

Please take few minutes to capture your initial thoughts and questions in your participant guide.

Wait for a few minutes so people can record their questions and insights before moving forward. By now, your participants should be familiar with the exercise and will be comfortable being alone with their own thoughts for a moment. When it appears that everyone has finished recording their thoughts, continue.

GRAPPLING

Let's take a second to evaluate how we're doing with our fearless discussions in general. During the first few weeks of the group, we emphasized how fearless conversations can only happen in a safe and respectful environment. We talked about the importance not only being good sharers but listeners also. So what do you think?

What are some of the things we do well as a group to promote fearless conversations? Allow for several responses.

Are there any areas you think we can grow as a group that would improve our discussions? Don't mention any names or specific incidents, just a positive reminder of a skill that would help us as a group.

Allow for responses.

Thanks for sharing your thoughts. Remember, we're all growing in this skill. Let's ask God to be in our conversation and to help guide us along.

Pray for the group, thanking God for the fantastic fearless conversation that has been shared up to this point. Ask God to show up again today, to direct the conversation so deeper friendships can be built and to help everyone understand him a little better.

LEADER LEARNING

By regularly allowing participants to give input on how well the group dynamics are going, you accomplish a few things. First, you're reminding them that this is their group, and they have ownership. Secondly, you're activating a means of getting feedback to the group members who need it in a safe and nonconfrontational way.

Let's get back into our small groups. You'll find three questions under the "Grappling" section of today's lesson. Start with just the first one. You'll talk about this for about 5 minutes in your small group, and then we'll hear some reports back to the larger group.

- **What risks were the crowds taking by singing that Jesus was the king who came in God's name? What do you think emboldened them to take this risk?**

Allow 5 minutes for discussion, and then have each group share something they feel is significant. Thank everyone for sharing.

Jesus response to the Pharisees was a clear indicator he had no intention of backing down. As a large group, let's talk about this:

- **What do you think was behind Jesus' comment that in this moment he would be declared King, even if the rocks needed to do the work?**

Allow time for different people to share their thoughts with the whole group. After a few minutes, thank everyone for sharing.

LEADER LEARNING

Do you find yourself with a participant who consistently overshares? Feel free to adapt the lesson to allow for more sharing within small groups. You'll limit the long-talker's influence and free up more participants to contribute to the group.

BEHIND THE SCENES

From our present-day vantage point and the benefit of hindsight, it's very easy for us to look at the Pharisees as the villains of the story. However, the Pharisees were viewed much more positively in Jesus' day. The Jews were living in the aftermath of Roman occupation as judgment for their disobedience to their covenant with God. The Pharisees, with their emphasis on rule keeping, were seen as the protectors of Israel's moral standing before God. In a sense, they were actively securing their country's national security. By strictly following God's rules, they hoped God would in turn renew the covenant and then intervene to remove Roman oppression.

Leader Guide

The worshiping crowds misunderstood Jesus by thinking he had come to unseat their oppressors. The Pharisees demonstrated they didn't understand who Jesus was through their constant opposition to his work. Jesus made a bold and calculated move by choosing to enter Jerusalem the way he did. Everyone was forced to make a decision about who they thought Jesus was. Do you think this is true today?

- **Is it possible for people have a "neutral" opinion about Jesus today? Why or why not?**

Allow time for different people to share their thoughts with the whole group. When several people have had a chance to respond, continue.

I want to have a chance for you to share in groups about your own observations and questions. Take time now to share anything that seemed especially relevant to you or any questions that came to mind as we read from Luke 19. Discuss those questions with your groups if you are willing to tackle them.

Allow at least 10 minutes for groups to talk. Give a 1-minute alert so people have time to finish their thoughts.

I hear a lot of good conversation in your groups. Does any group want to share an idea or a question that your group found interesting?

Allow a few minutes for different groups to share. Depending on how much time you have, allow each group to report their insights and unresolved questions to the larger group, or you can allow every group to respond to an insight or question that was shared.

GROWING

Our conversation was insightful and forced us to come to terms with just how outrageous Jesus' actions were. His processional forced everyone to form an opinion about just who this Jesus was. But it's a cautionary story, because even the people who claimed to follow Jesus misunderstood who he was.

There seems to be four responses to Jesus in this story. There were those who had a favorable opinion

of Jesus—the adoring crowds—who ended up not really grasping Jesus' mission. There were the Pharisees who refused to believe Jesus was their Messiah. In the background stood the Roman legions who had already dealt with the nuisance of other rebels who fancied themselves to be the rightful king of the Jews. All potential threats to Caesar were dealt with harshly. And finally, there were the citizens of Jerusalem, who were so busy going about their own business that they were unaware their King had come to visit them. But even so, the events of the week leading up to Jesus' death and resurrection would force everyone to form an opinion about this man who claimed to be their King.

This passage reminds us that we need to form an opinion about Jesus and who he is.

- **So where are you at? Are you like the crowds, who like the promise of Jesus so much that you are trying to enroll him in your cause? Are you like the Pharisees in that you aren't convinced Jesus is who he says he is? Or are you like the Romans who perceive Jesus as a threat to the way you like to rule your own life?**

Or perhaps you are like Jesus' disciples—you've committed to follow him, and you know you have more to learn about what he is truly like.

I invite you to take a hard and honest look at the options as you consider the truth of where you are in your life right now.

Invite everyone to write their reflections in the space provided in their participant guides. Let them know there's one more question for them there as well—they should go ahead and reflect on that question too.

Once you sense that people are wrapping up their work, close with a prayer, thanking God for the choice to accept Jesus as our good King.

LEADER GUIDE

LESSON 9: WHAT WAS REALLY GOING ON AT JESUS' "TRIUMPHAL ENTRY" INTO JERUSALEM? **85**

FEARLESS CONVERSATION

WHY IS JESUS SO RADICAL?

LESSON 10: WHAT IF GOD WANTS MORE THAN I WANT TO GIVE?

LEADER PREP

- Read the entire lesson ahead of time. Also read the corresponding pages in the Why Is Jesus So Radical? Participant Guide as there may be additional material provided there that may be helpful to you.

- Make yourself familiar with the "Behind the Scenes" boxes scattered throughout this lesson. If someone has a question, it's better to refer them to the guide than to provide the answer yourself. You'll help your group become comfortable with researching their own questions about the Bible when they are studying alone.

- Spend time talking to God about what he wants to teach you and the people in this class through today's lesson.

- Set a chair at the front of the room, facing people as they arrive. A child-sized chair is best, but any kind of chair will work.

GREETING

- Welcome everyone and be sure to introduce yourself.

- Be sure everyone has a copy of the participant guide.

- Let everyone know you'll be moving through Lesson 10 today, so they can find that section in the guide and use this to prompt them through today's lesson.

Leader Guide

- Explain that there are many "Behind the Scenes" commentary notes throughout the lesson. These can be read by participants as they come to that section of the lesson, or people who want to prepare ahead of time can read them during the week to prep for the next lesson.

Then say:

Did you ever have to sit in a "time-out" chair as a child? Remembering back to those days can get us thinking about the challenge of obeying—even when we don't want to. Think back to when you a kid—before your teen years. How easy of a child do you think you were to raise? Were you a compliant child? Or did you find yourself in the time-out chair more often than not? If you think you were fairly easy to raise and compliant most of the time, stand on this end of the room... indicate one side of the room. **If you think you were more on the "in trouble often" end of things as a child, stand at this end...** indicate the other side of the room.

Have everyone get up and stand on the side of the room that they think best fit them as a child. It's okay if people place themselves somewhere in the middle of the room as well. When everyone has found a spot, have people form groups of two or three with those nearby and share why they stood in this location. Allow about 3 minutes for talking.

Okay, now I want you to remember what you were like when you were a teenager. Of course, you outgrew the time-out chair by then. But how easy was it to obey your parents during those years? Rate yourself during your teen years from being an "angel" to being...well, far from being an angel. Again indicate sides of the room and have everyone move again to a new location based on their self-assessments. This time ask people to only form groups of two and share with a partner as to why they rated themselves this way.

For this next question, have your pair join with another pair to form a small group. Go ahead and find a place to sit together as this will be your small group for today. Once you're seated, discuss the first question for today's lesson.

- **What house rules were the hardest for you to obey when you were growing up? Why?**

Allow the participants a few minutes to share with each other. When you sense the sharing is slowing down, continue.

We got to know each other a little better by sharing a small slice of our childhoods. You know, most children want to please their parents. But as we all know from experience, it's hard to obey when we don't want to. We're about to explore a time when Jesus experienced this same struggle...but he struggled to obey his Father when he was an adult!

BEHIND THE SCENES

Today's passage is a study in contrasts between Jesus and his disciples and how well they obeyed. God wanted more from them than they wanted to give. Jesus was aware he was about to be betrayed at the hand of Judas, an event that would ultimately lead to his death on the cross and his experiencing separation from his Heavenly Father. The latter consequence was infinitely more severe than the first. From eternity, Jesus was a member of the Trinity and experienced a perfect and intimate relationship with the Father and the Holy Spirit. This closeness would be broken when Jesus bore the sins of the world. When Jesus hung on the cross, he responded to this alienation by asking why God had forsaken him.

Before then, in the Garden of Gethsemane, Jesus bore the anxiety that came with anticipating his fate. He asked Peter, James, and John to join him in prayer as he asked God for the strength to obey. In this time of prayer, Jesus wasn't shrinking from his impending death. Instead, he suffered knowing that he alone would bear God's anger that the world earned due to its sinfulness. Jesus asked God to take this burden from him, but he qualified his request by adding he would surrender to God's will instead of his own.

GROUNDING

Let's get grounded in God's Word, so we can understand how to respond when God calls us to do something we don't want to do. Today's Bible account is from Matthew 26:36-55. Matthew stressed throughout his Gospel how Jesus carefully fulfilled the Old Testament prophecies about him in order to break the power of sin. However, in this passage, the price of obeying his Father in order to accomplish salvation is impossibly high. Let's dig in.

Pray for the group to be receptive to hear God speaking through his Word and through their fellow group members. Ask God to help you all discover how to become obedient to him, even when we don't want to.

LEADER LEARNING

If you discover you have a group member who is overly quiet and doesn't contribute, be sure to affirm his or her sharing when they do share. You might even make that affirmation outside the group if you sense

LESSON 10: WHAT IF GOD WANTS MORE THAN I WANT TO GIVE?

public attention would be unwanted. Think twice before you call on that person to share if they don't volunteer. You might create an awkward moment that will make future sharing even more difficult.

Read Matthew 26:36-55 aloud, or invite a few volunteers to read a few paragraphs each until the entire passage has been read. Encourage everyone to follow along in their Bibles or their participant guides.

God's Word: Matthew 26:36-55

36 Then Jesus went with them to the olive grove called Gethsemane, and he said, "Sit here while I go over there to pray." 37 He took Peter and Zebedee's two sons, James and John, and he became anguished and distressed. 38 He told them, "My soul is crushed with grief to the point of death. Stay here and keep watch with me."

39 He went on a little farther and bowed with his face to the ground, praying, "My Father! If it is possible, let this cup of suffering be taken away from me. Yet I want your will to be done, not mine."

40 Then he returned to the disciples and found them asleep. He said to Peter, "Couldn't you watch with me even one hour? 41 Keep watch and pray, so that you will not give in to temptation. For the spirit is willing, but the body is weak!"

42 Then Jesus left them a second time and prayed, "My Father! If this cup cannot be taken away unless I drink it, your will be done." 43 When he returned to them again, he found them sleeping, for they couldn't keep their eyes open.

44 So he went to pray a third time, saying the same things again. 45 Then he came to the disciples and said, "Go ahead and sleep. Have your rest. But look—the time has come. The Son of Man is betrayed into the hands of sinners. 46 Up, let's be going. Look, my betrayer is here!"

47 While he was still speaking, Judas, one of the Twelve, arrived. With him was a large crowd armed with swords and clubs, sent from the chief priests and the elders of the people. 48 Now the betrayer had arranged a signal with them: "The one I kiss is the man; arrest him." 49 Going at once to Jesus, Judas said, "Greetings, Rabbi!" and kissed him.

50 Jesus replied, "Do what you came for, friend."

Then the men stepped forward, seized Jesus and arrested him. 51 With that, one of Jesus' companions reached for his sword, drew it out and struck the servant of the high priest, cutting off his ear. ▶

> ⁵² "Put your sword back in its place," Jesus said to him, "for all who draw the sword will die by the sword. ⁵³ Do you think I cannot call on my Father, and he will at once put at my disposal more than twelve legions of angels? ⁵⁴ But how then would the Scriptures be fulfilled that say it must happen in this way?"
>
> ⁵⁵ In that hour Jesus said to the crowd, "Am I leading a rebellion, that you have come out with swords and clubs to capture me? Every day I sat in the temple courts teaching, and you did not arrest me."

Before we discuss this let's take a moment to reflect.

- **What questions come to mind and what catches your attention in this passage?**

I'd like you to capture those initial thoughts and questions in your participant guide.

Wait a few minutes so people can write out their thoughts and questions before moving forward. Stress that this isn't the time to discuss the passage with others. It's best to react to the passage alone first.

When it appears that everyone is ready to move on, continue.

GRAPPLING

We'll get to those questions and thoughts you just wrote down in a bit. But let's grapple with a few other questions first. Before we start our time of discussion, let me ask you a question: At the end of this lesson, how will know if you participated in a good fearless conversation?

Allow for several responses. Be sure to model listening and affirmation skills as you take their responses. After several people have had a chance to respond, continue.

Those are some strong indicators of a healthy and enjoyable fearless conversation. Let's do our best to practice those things now, so we can be satisfied with our work at the end of the lesson.

We'll continue discussing in our small groups. Find the first question under the "Grappling" section of Lesson 10. You'll talk about this first question for about 5 minutes in your group, and then we'll hear some reports back to the larger group.

LESSON 10: WHAT IF GOD WANTS MORE THAN I WANT TO GIVE?

Leader Guide

- **Jesus was fully God yet still struggled to want to obey his Father. In what ways does that remind you of yourself?**

Allow about 5 minutes for discussion, and then have each group share something they feel is significant. Thank everyone for sharing.

LEADER LEARNING

One way to keep people returning from week to week is for you as the leader to make some sort of contact with each participant during the week. It can be a phone call, an email, a text, or a personal note sent in the mail (a rare thing indeed). The contact should be positive and brief, such as, "Hi! Just wanted to check in with you and let you know that I appreciated your insights and humor in our last lesson. I hope you'll be able to come next time—our group really appreciates you. Let me know if I can pray for you or help in any other way." This contact helps participants know you're concerned for them beyond the one hour you have with them in the lesson.

BEHIND THE SCENES

Throughout the Bible, the number "three" signifies completeness. Jesus wrestled with God in prayer three times and completely surrendered to God. The disciples surrendered to sleep three times and were completely unprepared to resist the temptation to resist arrest through violence.

Let's tackle this next question as a large group.

- **What difference does it make whether the disciples were asleep or not, given the certainty of Jesus' arrest and crucifixion?**

Allow about 5 minutes for discussion—have people call out their thoughts to the entire group. When the sharing has concluded, continue.

Jesus chose three close friends to take with him to pray. He pulled them aside and said, "My soul is overwhelmed with sorrow to the point of death. Stay here and keep watch with me." It's interesting that even Jesus needed close friends, especially at this time of intense grief. This reminds us how important it is for us to have friends who can come alongside us in difficult times.

It's likely that many of us here are struggling in some area of life. Life is messy and full of complexities. Even if we're not crushed with grief, we still need friends to support us in difficult times.

Let's take time right now for fearless conversations in our small groups where we are open about our lives

92 FEARLESS CONVERSATION: **WHY IS JESUS SO RADICAL?**

and the need we have for prayer. As much as you are comfortable, share in your small group and pray for each other. You don't have to go into great detail—just briefly share and then pray together. You'll have about 5 minutes.

After this time of sharing and prayer, have people return their attention to you and continue. Note that if some groups are still in prayer, it's okay to let them keep praying as you speak quietly and direct everyone else to continue with the lesson.

Let's keep talking in our small groups. This is your opportunity to share your own observations and questions about the passage. Take time now to share anything that seemed especially relevant to you when we read from Matthew 26. If your group is willing, you can try to tackle some of those big questions.

Allow at least 10 minutes for groups to talk. Give a 1-minute "time to wrap it up!" alert so groups have time to finish their thoughts.

Does any group want to share an idea or a question you found interesting?

Allow a few minutes for different groups to share. Depending on how much time you have remaining, you can choose to either let groups take turns reporting back their insights and questions, or you can invite the larger group to respond to a single insight or question that was shared.

GROWING

Fearless conversations are fantastic in that they allow us to understand the importance of being obedient to God even when we don't want to. But we need to remember that *intending* to obey God when it's hard isn't the same thing as actually *doing* it.

In the passage immediately preceding the one we just read, Peter argues with Jesus and says he would remain faithful to Jesus, even though Jesus says Peter will deny him three times. And, if we were to read ahead, we'd see that Peter doesn't obey Jesus any better than the other disciples.

We all have some areas in our life where it's relatively easy to follow Jesus. For some of you being generous or being hospitable is

LESSON 10: WHAT IF GOD WANTS MORE THAN I WANT TO GIVE?   93

Leader Guide

easy. Some of you can talk about your faith in God easily. We all have our areas of strength.

But we also have areas in our life where we just don't want to obey God. Perhaps you've heard a prompting from God to do something specific and you just don't want to take that risk. Or perhaps there's a sinful pattern in your life that you just don't want to turn over to God.

Jesus did something bold. He trusted his Father enough to tell him that he didn't want to obey, even while affirming that he would. He had confidence in his Father's character to trust him with this honesty. We're going to take a moment and have a fearless conversation with our Heavenly Father in the privacy of our participant guides. There are a couple of questions for your own reflection, and a place to write out a prayer to God about an area in your life where you find it difficult to obey him.

Invite everyone to write their reflections in the space provided in their participant guides. Let them know there is one more question for them there as well—they should read and reflect on that question too.

Allow time for people to adequately reflect and journal; then close with a prayer, thanking God that we can be honest about our struggles with obeying him.

94   FEARLESS CONVERSATION: **WHY IS JESUS SO RADICAL?**

FEARLESS CONVERSATION

WHY IS JESUS SO RADICAL?

LESSON 11: DID GOD REALLY DISOWN JESUS ON THE CROSS?

LEADER PREP

- Read the entire lesson ahead of time. Also read the corresponding pages in the Why Is Jesus So Radical? Participant Guide as there may be additional material provided there that may be helpful to you.

- Make yourself especially familiar with the "Behind the Scenes" boxes scattered throughout this lesson. If someone has a question, it's better to refer them to the guide than to provide the answer yourself. You'll help your group become comfortable with researching their own questions about the Bible when they are studying alone.

- Pray. Lots.

GREETING

- Welcome everyone and be sure to introduce yourself.

- Be sure everyone has a copy of the participant guide.

- Let everyone know you'll be moving through Lesson 11 today, so they can find that section in the guide and use this to prompt them through today's lesson.

- Explain that there are many "Behind the Scenes" commentary notes throughout the lesson. These can be read by participants as they come to that section of the lesson—or people

Leader Guide

who want to prepare ahead of time can read them during the week to be ready for the next lesson.

Begin by asking:

Thinking back to your high school years, what were some of the stereotypes that people got grouped into at your school? What were those labels? Jocks? Geeks? What else?

Give people a few minutes to call out their responses to the large group.

Let's get into groups of no more than four and continue our discussion about how people end up in certain groups. Talk about the group with which you most closely identified when you were growing up. There are a few questions on this topic in your participant guide for you to discuss.

- **What group did you most associate with in high school, and why?**

- **Was being labeled as a part of this group positive, or did you feel like an outcast in this group? Explain your answer.**

Allow about 5 minutes for people to get into small groups and discuss the questions. Then have everyone return their attention to you.

Thanks for sharing in your groups. Today we're going to be grappling with the labels that were applied to Jesus and how he responded to the harsh rejection associated with those labels.

GROUNDING

We're going to read a passage from Matthew 27, but before we do I'd like to pray for us that God will guide this time we have together. Let's pray.

Ask God to guide the conversations in each group. Trust that the Holy Spirit will take each discussion in the way it needs to go.

Read Matthew 27:32-55 aloud, or ask for a volunteer to read today's passage aloud. Have people follow along in their own Bibles or in their participant guides.

96 FEARLESS CONVERSATION: **WHY IS JESUS SO RADICAL?**

God's Word: Matthew 27:32-55

³² As they were going out, they met a man from Cyrene, named Simon, and they forced him to carry the cross. ³³ They came to a place called Golgotha (which means "the place of the skull"). ³⁴ There they offered Jesus wine to drink, mixed with gall; but after tasting it, he refused to drink it. ³⁵ When they had crucified him, they divided up his clothes by casting lots. ³⁶ And sitting down, they kept watch over him there. ³⁷ Above his head they placed the written charge against him: THIS IS JESUS, THE KING OF THE JEWS.

³⁸ Two rebels were crucified with him, one on his right and one on his left. ³⁹ Those who passed by hurled insults at him, shaking their heads ⁴⁰ and saying, "You who are going to destroy the temple and build it in three days, save yourself! Come down from the cross, if you are the Son of God!" ⁴¹ In the same way the chief priests, the teachers of the law and the elders mocked him. ⁴² "He saved others," they said, "but he can't save himself! He's the king of Israel! Let him come down now from the cross, and we will believe in him. ⁴³ He trusts in God. Let God rescue him now if he wants him, for he said, 'I am the Son of God.'" ⁴⁴ In the same way the rebels who were crucified with him also heaped insults on him.

⁴⁵ From noon until three in the afternoon darkness came over all the land. ⁴⁶ About three in the afternoon Jesus cried out in a loud voice, *"Eli, Eli, lema sabachthani?"* (which means "My God, my God, why have you forsaken me?")

⁴⁷ When some of those standing there heard this, they said, "He's calling Elijah."

⁴⁸ Immediately one of them ran and got a sponge. He filled it with wine vinegar, put it on a staff, and offered it to Jesus to drink. ⁴⁹ The rest said, "Now leave him alone. Let's see if Elijah comes to save him."

⁵⁰ And when Jesus had cried out again in a loud voice, he gave up his spirit.

⁵¹ At that moment the curtain of the temple was torn in two from top to bottom. The earth shook, the rocks split ⁵² and the tombs broke open. The bodies of many holy people who had died were raised to life. ⁵³ They came out of the tombs after Jesus' resurrection and went into the holy city and appeared to many people.

⁵⁴ When the centurion and those with him who were guarding Jesus saw the earthquake and all that had happened, they were terrified, and exclaimed, "Surely he was the Son of God!"

⁵⁵ Many women were there, watching from a distance. They had followed Jesus from Galilee to care for his needs.

LESSON 11: DID GOD REALLY DISOWN JESUS ON THE CROSS?

Leader Guide

Let's take a moment to reflect on what we just read.

• **When you read this passage, what jumps out at you and grabs your attention?**

Write down your initial thoughts and questions in your participant guide.

Give people a few minutes to jot down their questions or thoughts before moving forward. This should be something that people do on their own, not in discussion groups. When everyone looks like they're ready, continue.

GRAPPLING

As we begin our time of discussion, let's remember this is a safe place for sharing and conversation, especially when we're talking about rejection and how Jesus responded to rejection in his own life. This means we will be respectful, not interrupt, and consider the different opinions of others.

LEADER LEARNING

When you start dealing with sensitive topics like rejection, it may be difficult to get people to open up. They're not sure just how vulnerable they're supposed to be. Address this problem by demonstrating an appropriate level of vulnerability in your own stories. When the members of the group hear your example, they'll have a better idea of how deep to go and perhaps find the courage to go there.

BEHIND THE SCENES

The word *excruciating* comes from the same root word for crucifixion—and for good reason. This finely-tuned method of torture and execution had been perfected by the Romans to maximize the mental, emotional, and physical agony of the condemned person. It was not uncommon for the Romans to crucify more than one person at a time. In fact, the roads leading up to Jerusalem had hundreds of crosses along them, set apart like telephone poles, with those being crucified at various stages of death—the process of which would sometimes last for days.

The public display of a crucified man was meant to maximize the humiliation of this person, who had been stripped and then roped and nailed to a wooden beam, which had already been stained with the blood and bodily fluids of previous victims. There is simply no more agonizing picture of the total rejection of a human being than to crucify that individual during this time in history. The ultimate cruelty of crucifixion was the creation of a state of complete hopelessness in the victim.

There were two contrasting reactions to Jesus' crucifixion: the first was the sarcasm, mockery, and taunting of Jesus with humiliating accusations; the other response was one of compassion and acknowledgment of his innocence. Many of those who mocked him may have been cheering him on when he rode into Jerusalem on a donkey. The religious leaders kept throwing Jesus' words back at him at a time when he was the most vulnerable. In contrast, when the other disciples had scattered, John and Mary, the mother of Jesus, stuck around despite how horrifying this must have been for them.

Even if you've read this portion of the Bible before, it is a very emotional scene and is hard to read without a reaction. Let's share some of those thoughts with the larger group.

- **What kind of gut reaction do you have when you read the account of Jesus' crucifixion?**

Allow several people to share their thoughts and reactions with the larger group. Feel free to share your own response as well.

As we grapple with this question, think back on your conversations about being labeled a certain way in high school. For some of us this may have been a time of feeling rejected. Perhaps you even identify with those feelings today as an adult. Consider those emotions as you think about the rejection that Jesus was experiencing on the cross.

- **How do you think the crowd's reaction to Jesus' crucifixion would have added to his sense of humiliation and rejection?**

Allow time for different people to share their thoughts with the whole group. Remember to model and encourage listening and respect for others as they share. When several people have had a chance to respond, continue.

I'd like us to have a chance to share in our small groups about our own insights and questions. Take time now to share anything that seemed especially relevant to you as we read from Matthew 27. Talk about some of the questions that popped into your mind.

LESSON 11: DID GOD REALLY DISOWN JESUS ON THE CROSS? 99

Leader Guide

Allow at least 10 minutes for groups to talk. Give a 1-minute warning so groups have time to finish their thoughts.

Does any group want to share an idea or a question that your group found interesting?

Allow a few minutes for different groups to share. Depending on how much time you have left you can simply let groups report their insights and questions, or if you have time you can invite the larger group to respond to an insight or question that was shared.

LEADER LEARNING

Spiritual growth is sometimes messy and often mysterious. Some issues may not get fully resolved in this session, and that's okay. Encourage people to dig into these issues outside of class, perhaps with a trusted Christian over a cup of coffee.

BEHIND THE SCENES

Matthew's account of the Crucifixion gives us clues about what happened to Jesus without explicitly saying so. Jesus needed help carrying the cross, probably because his whipping had been so severe his shredded muscles simply couldn't bear the weight of the beam. Jesus refused the gall-infused wine because it was used as a painkiller for the crucified, one of the few merciful options offered to those who were about to die in this hideous manner. Jesus refused the sedative, likely because he needed to bear the full brunt of the sacrifice he made willingly. The fact that the soldiers were divvying up his clothes tells us that Jesus was probably stripped down to his loin cloth or was even naked, again to increase the humiliation of the experience.

In the midst of all this pain and suffering and rejection, there were miracles that could not have gone unnoticed. Look back through the Bible passage and consider the miracles that are mentioned. In your small group, talk about those and why they were important.

- **What do you think was the significance of all the miraculous events that occurred in the moments surrounding Christ's death?**

After about 5 minutes of discussion in small groups, invite a few people to share their insights with the larger group. Then continue.

So did God really forsake Jesus on the cross? Some Bible scholars say that God had to forsake Jesus so that Jesus could fully atone for, or make amends, for our sins. In a sense, God the Father had to turn

100 FEARLESS CONVERSATION: WHY IS JESUS SO RADICAL?

his back on Jesus when the sin of the world was upon him. Jesus certainly bore the full emotional brunt of God turning away from him. You have to wonder if this was even worse than all the physical suffering that came along with crucifixion.

BEHIND THE SCENES

Matthew calls attention to the detail that the curtain in the Temple, which protected the Holy of Holies, was torn from top to bottom—and not the reverse. From this the reader can conclude that it was God doing the tearing (not two people at the bottom pulling the two sides apart). With the curtain torn in two, people now had full access to the Holy of Holies, which represented God's presence.

What do you think is the connection between God tearing this curtain in two and Jesus' atoning work on the cross?

GROWING

What does this all mean for our lives? I think we can look to the response of one group of people who were at this incredible event for insights. In verse 54 we read, "When the centurion and those with him who were guarding Jesus saw the earthquake and all that had happened, they were terrified, and exclaimed, 'Surely he was the Son of God!'"

Their response was one of terror but also one of acknowledgement that Jesus truly was the Son of God. We don't have to be terrified, but we can acknowledge who Jesus is and what this means to us.

Take the last few minutes of our time together to reflect on the last two questions in your participant guide. This is your own time for reflection and application.

Allow time for people to adequately reflect and journal; then close with a prayer, thanking God for bringing Jesus through the crucifixion.

LESSON 11: DID GOD REALLY DISOWN JESUS ON THE CROSS?

FEARLESS CONVERSATION

WHY IS JESUS SO RADICAL?

LESSON 12: RESURRECTION SEEMS SO IMPOSSIBLE... HOW CAN I BELIEVE IN A LITERAL "EASTER" STORY?

LEADER PREP

- Read the entire lesson ahead of time. Also read the corresponding pages in the Why Is Jesus So Radical? Participant Guide as there may be additional material provided there that may be helpful to you.

- Make yourself especially familiar with the "Behind the Scenes" boxes scattered throughout this lesson. If someone has a question, it's better to refer them to the guide than to provide the answer yourself. You'll help your group become comfortable with researching their own questions about the Bible when they are studying alone.

- Pray. Lots.

FOR EXTRA IMPACT
Bring along a few pieces of paper currency (like a few dollar bills) and some play money from a board game.

Prep Notes:

GREETING

- Welcome everyone and be sure to introduce yourself.

- Be sure everyone has a copy of the participant guide.

- Let everyone know you'll be moving through Lesson 12 today, so they can find that section in the guide and use this to prompt them through today's lesson.

- Explain that there are many "Behind the Scenes" commentary notes throughout the lesson. These can be read by participants as they come to that section of the lesson—or people who want to prepare ahead of time can read them during the week to be prepared for the next lesson.

Begin by bringing out your play money and real money if you brought those, and use them as you ask the first question. If you didn't bring these, adapt the questions a bit to get to the same conclusion.

If I want to buy something at your garage sale and I offer you these as payment (hold up the pretend money), **how would you respond?**

Hear a few responses from the group.

So you want this instead? Hold up the real money. **How do you know the difference?**

You can expect a few smirks about the obvious answers, but that's okay. Give people a minute to share their responses with the larger group.

In the case of real money versus pretend money, what I've brought today is super obvious as to what is real and what isn't. But some people are so adept at making fake money that they even fool experts.

Let's get into groups of no more than four and talk about how to distinguish what is real from what is fake—or how to tell the truth from a lie.

Have everyone move into groups of four, moving their chairs as needed to accomplish this. Have them turn to pages 81 and 82 in their participant guides and discuss the questions there that relate to real and fake.

- **What do you think you're good at recognizing as a fake? Money?**

Artwork? Watches? Designer clothing? How do you know something is fake?

Sometimes the differences are obvious like with our currency. But sometimes it's a lot harder to tell what's real and what's false, like when someone shares a rumor with you that seems plausible.

- **Tell about a time you heard a rumor and, for at least a while, you believed it was true. What made the rumor so believable at the time?**

Allow about 8 minutes for people to discuss these questions. Give a 30-second "time to wrap it up!" warning. Then have everyone return their attention to you.

Thanks for sharing in your groups. Today we're going to be looking at the false stories that were broadcast to explain away the Resurrection and how we can fearlessly converse about what happened when Jesus rose from the dead.

Just about every day we're given the opportunity to choose between what is real and what is not. We might not be given fake money, but through advertising, news stories, bits of stories passed along through the Internet, and so on, we hear a lot of lies. Some of these are easy to discern, as some of them are meant to make us laugh—such as a funny advertisement that stretches the truth to make us remember a product. But sometimes it's hard to know what to believe. Who really said what and when and why?

Distinguishing between truth and error when it comes to the resurrection of Jesus is absolutely crucial when it comes to believing the claims of Christ. The validity of our Christian faith stands on the belief that the resurrection of Christ is a verifiable, historical event.

GROUNDING

Let's read the account of the Resurrection from Matthew and pay attention to the details of everything that went on. But first, let's pray.

If anyone has doubts about what happened on the third day after Jesus' resurrection, this lesson provides an ideal opportunity to express those doubts so that they can be addressed. Ask the Lord to guide the conversations in each group and to reveal a little more of himself through today's lesson.

LESSON 12: RESURRECTION SEEMS SO IMPOSSIBLE...HOW CAN I BELIEVE IN A LITERAL "EASTER" STORY?

Read Matthew 27:62–28:15, or ask for a volunteer to read today's passage aloud. Encourage everyone else to follow along in their own Bibles or in their participant guides.

God's Word: Matthew 27:62-28:15

⁶² The next day, the one after Preparation Day, the chief priests and the Pharisees went to Pilate. ⁶³ "Sir," they said, "we remember that while he was still alive that deceiver said, 'After three days I will rise again.' ⁶⁴ So give the order for the tomb to be made secure until the third day. Otherwise, his disciples may come and steal the body and tell the people that he has been raised from the dead. This last deception will be worse than the first."

⁶⁵ "Take a guard," Pilate answered. "Go, make the tomb as secure as you know how." ⁶⁶ So they went and made the tomb secure by putting a seal on the stone and posting the guard.

28 ¹ After the Sabbath, at dawn on the first day of the week, Mary Magdalene and the other Mary went to look at the tomb.

² There was a violent earthquake, for an angel of the Lord came down from heaven and, going to the tomb, rolled back the stone and sat on it. ³ His appearance was like lightning, and his clothes were white as snow. ⁴ The guards were so afraid of him that they shook and became like dead men.

⁵ The angel said to the women, "Do not be afraid, for I know that you are looking for Jesus, who was crucified. ⁶ He is not here; he has risen, just as he said. Come and see the place where he lay. ⁷ Then go quickly and tell his disciples: 'He has risen from the dead and is going ahead of you into Galilee. There you will see him.' Now I have told you."

⁸ So the women hurried away from the tomb, afraid yet filled with joy, and ran to tell his disciples. ⁹ Suddenly Jesus met them. "Greetings," he said. They came to him, clasped his feet and worshiped him. ¹⁰ Then Jesus said to them, "Do not be afraid. Go and tell my brothers to go to Galilee; there they will see me."

¹¹ While the women were on their way, some of the guards went into the city and reported to the chief priests everything that had happened. ¹² When the chief priests had met with the elders and devised a plan, they gave the soldiers a large

sum of money, [13] telling them, "You are to say, 'His disciples came during the night and stole him away while we were asleep.' [14] If this report gets to the governor, we will satisfy him and keep you out of trouble." [15] So the soldiers took the money and did as they were instructed. And this story has been widely circulated among the Jews to this very day."

Let's take a moment to reflect on this passage.

- **What questions come to mind? What catches your attention?**

Write down those initial thoughts and questions in your participant guide.

Give people a few minutes to jot down their questions or thoughts before moving forward. This should be something that people do on their own, not in groups. When everyone looks like they're finished, move on.

GRAPPLING

Before we start into this time of discussion, let's remember that this is a safe place to express our doubts and to ask questions. This means we will be respectful, not interrupt, and consider the perspectives of others.

LEADER LEARNING

Sometimes people in church settings will hesitate to ask questions that imply that they might not be 100 percent on board with the church's statement of faith. They want to belong, so they just don't rock the boat by bringing up their doubts. Reassure the people in your group that asking the hard questions and grappling with those issues is really the only way to strengthen our faith. Perhaps you might want to talk about a time when you were able to resolve certain doubts by fearlessly grappling with the matter at hand. So be sure to offer an open invitation to ask any question and to put any issue on the table.

Let's discuss this passage about the Resurrection in our small groups. Find the first question under the "Grappling" section of your participant guide. Talk about that first question for about 5 minutes in your small group, and then we'll hear some reports back to the larger group.

- **What problems did the religious leaders who pushed for Jesus' crucifixion believe his death would**

LESSON 12: RESURRECTION SEEMS SO IMPOSSIBLE...HOW CAN I BELIEVE IN A LITERAL "EASTER" STORY?

solve? What problems did they discover still remained?

Allow about 5 minutes for discussion, and then have each group share something they feel is significant. Encourage people to focus on the historical details in the biblical account.

Let's talk about this next question as a large group. When we hear of something that seems unbelievable, we often ask about who saw this or who was there when it happened. We want to add the credibility of the witnesses to our decision about whether or not to believe what we've just heard. Remember that we are just reading Matthew's account—the Resurrection story is told many times in the Bible. But even with this one account, we read of a number of people being involved.

- What do you think is the importance of establishing more than one eyewitness here?

Allow time for different people to share their thoughts with the whole group. When several people have had a chance to respond, continue.

I'd like us to have a chance to share in our groups about our own insights and questions. Take time now to share anything that seemed especially relevant to you as we read from Matthew 27. Talk about some of the questions that popped into your mind.

Allow at least 10 minutes for groups to talk. Give a 1-minute alert so groups have time to finish their thoughts.

Does any group want to share an idea or a question that your group found interesting?

Allow a few minutes for different groups to share. Depending on how much time you have left you can simply let groups report their insights and questions, or if you have time you can invite the larger group to respond to an insight or question that was shared.

LEADER LEARNING

Some of your participants may be having doubts but they're not sure how to articulate them. Better to get them out in the open, however, then to let them go unspoken. Perhaps a safe way to do this is to ask participants to speculate how the first people hearing the fabricated stories of the religious leaders may have reacted. That way, people get to express their doubts "hypothetically" instead of attributing those questions to themselves.

BEHIND THE SCENES

Even the enemies of Jesus remembered his prediction that after three days he would rise from the dead. So the religious leaders and the Romans took every precaution to be certain that the disciples (who were hiding in fear for their own lives) wouldn't sneak in and steal the body. Pilate gave instructions to make the tomb as secure as possible. This meant a seal and a guard. If anyone attempted to break a Roman seal without authorization, that person would be crucified immediately. The guards themselves would be crucified if they allowed anyone to do it without a fight to the death. In fact, tradition tells us that the soldiers guarding the tomb were crucified themselves for failing to keep Jesus' body in the tomb.

As Jesus reminded Pilate, the governor would have no authority unless it had been given to him by God. So God had no problem superseding the authority of the Roman seal and telling his angelic messengers to simply go break it so that the Risen Christ could walk out of the tomb unhindered. After the Resurrection, Jesus simply appeared and disappeared, so he probably didn't need the stone rolled away.

But those who would be the first witnesses of the Resurrection certainly did.

What do you think? Did God really raise Jesus from the dead? The religious leaders and the Romans went to great lengths to ensure that Jesus' prediction of his resurrection couldn't be fabricated in any way.

- **Why might reasonable people believe Jesus literally rose from the dead? Why might reasonable people doubt that happened?**

Invite people to share their thoughts with the rest of the group. It can take courage to express doubt in a room filled with Christians, so be honoring to those who are still unsure what to believe. This is a great place to show them grace and love instead of getting into an arguing match.

BEHIND THE SCENES

More than likely, the two Marys followed the angel's instructions, stepping over the heavily armed unconscious guards and looking into the tomb to find it empty. If the women had arrived any earlier, they would have probably been cut down immediately by the guards whose own lives were at stake if any follower of Jesus came anywhere near the tomb.

When the women at the tomb first saw Jesus they clung to his feet. Given Jesus' response, they have may done this in part to make sure he wasn't going anywhere! However, Jesus told them that it was okay, he wasn't leaving yet, and to go tell the disciples to meet him in Galilee, about 63 miles to the north.

GROWING

Once we get to the point where we believe that the resurrection of Christ was an actual, historical event, we can grapple with the impact that the event has on our lives and in strengthening our faith.

There were two stories circulating in Bible times about why there was no body in Jesus' tomb on the third day after his crucifixion. The first tale was that the disciples came and stole the body—that somehow they emerged from hiding, snuck by the well-trained guards, rolled away the stone on their own, took the body, and then fabricated the entire Christian faith (an apparent lie for which all but one of them probably died a martyr's death).

The second story was that Jesus was really alive again, and he offered a multitude of evidence to back that up.

You have to decide which of these two possibilities you believe—or if you believe another solution that you've heard along the way. What you believe regarding this event is key to your relationship with God.

The people we've read about today had a variety of responses. Some responded in fear, others with joy. Some shared the good news, some tried to squelch it. Where are you in this mix?

Take time to reflect on the remaining questions for today's lesson. You'll have time to write your personal thoughts during this time.

- Where do you find yourself in this question of belief? Do you believe Jesus rose from the dead, or is there another explanation you believe explains Jesus' missing body?

- How do you respond to people who are not sure that the resurrection of Christ actually happened?

- Throughout this quarter we've been asking the question, Why is Jesus so radical? What was radical about Jesus being dead, and then being alive again three days later? In what sense does the Resurrection validate the truthfulness of everything Jesus ever said or did?

Allow time for people to adequately reflect and journal; then close with a prayer, thanking God for raising Jesus from the dead—and making that event central to everything we believe as Christians.

FEARLESS CONVERSATION

WHY IS JESUS SO RADICAL?

LESSON 13: HOW CAN I KNOW JESUS IS REALLY ALIVE TODAY?

LEADER PREP

- Read the entire lesson ahead of time. Also read the corresponding pages in the Why Is Jesus So Radical? Participant Guide as there may be additional material provided there that may be helpful to you.

- Make yourself familiar with the "Behind the Scenes" boxes scattered throughout this lesson. If someone has a question, it's better to refer them to the guide than to provide the answer yourself. You'll help your group become comfortable with researching their own questions about the Bible when they are studying alone.

- Collect a variety of small objects that represent different textures, such as a sponge, eraser, block of wood, a plastic ball, sandpaper, and so on. Before anyone has seen the objects, cover them with a towel so no one can see what they are.

- Pray for this last lesson of the quarter to touch hearts and keep people engaged in conversations that can be life changing.

Prep Notes:

LEADER GUIDE

GREETING

- Welcome everyone and be sure to introduce yourself.

- Be sure everyone has a copy of the participant guide.

- Let everyone know you'll be moving through Lesson 13 today, so they can find that section in the guide and use it to prompt them through today's lesson.

- Explain that there are many "Behind the Scenes" commentary notes throughout the lesson. These can be read by participants as they come to that section of the lesson—or people can read them during the week to prep ahead of time.

- Have copies of the participant guide for the next quarter of Fearless Conversation handy so everyone can see what's coming next!

Begin by having everyone get into groups of no more than four people. Invite participants to move their chairs so they can easily sit with their group and to be sure and introduce themselves to each other.

I'd like the person wearing the most red in your group to come over to this table where I have some hidden objects. This person will select one item (and I promise that nothing here is disgusting or gross!) and take that back to his or her group. The rest of the group will try to identify that object just by touching it—so that means you'll have to close your eyes!

Have those wearing the most red come up and select any item from the collection you have, while everyone else closes their eyes. Have the red-wearing group take their items back and hold them so that everyone in their group can easily touch the item. See how quickly each group can identify their item. Once they've guessed correctly they may open their eyes and the item can be returned to the table. Choose a different person from each group to choose a new item, and repeat the activity once more.

For this activity you clearly relied most heavily on your sense of touch. Did you use any other senses—taste, hearing, or smell—to help you? If so, which ones?

Invite anyone who has something to share to do so. Then continue.

112 FEARLESS CONVERSATION: WHY IS JESUS SO RADICAL?

Our senses help us make sense of the world around us. Let's talk about those a bit in our small groups. You'll find a question to discuss in your participant guide. Talk for about 4 minutes with your small group.

- **Which one of your senses—sight, taste, touch, hearing, or smell—do you think you rely on most? If you had to lose one sense, which one would you choose to lose? (And if you've ever lost a sense, you're invited to share about that!)**

Allow 4 or 5 minutes for discussion. Be sensitive to the fact that some people may have experienced losing a sense for a time or perhaps permanently. Don't make anyone feel put on the spot.

Thanks for tackling that question. We constantly use our five senses to tell us what's true and real. We used touch to determine what the objects were that we were handed. We use sight to decide if we're driving too close to the car in front of us. We use smell to decide if the milk is sour or not.

But what happens when your senses tell you something can't possibly be true—yet it is? When Jesus' followers first saw him after his resurrection, Jesus offered them physical evidence he was alive. They could touch, see, and hear him. But what about today? How can we know that Jesus is alive? How can we know what's true?

Usually we decide if something is true based on a variety of factors. We use our senses, we look at the evidence, we rely on our past experiences, and so on. But when Jesus disappeared from his tomb there was nothing for the people in Jerusalem to touch—just a question that demanded an answer. What had happened? How we—and others—answer that question has huge implications.

GROUNDING

Let's read the account of what happened after the Resurrection and how Jesus convinced his disciples he was really back from the dead (in his glorified body). Whatever he did or said, once his disciples experienced it they no longer doubted.

Be aware that even among those who self-identify as Christians, there are those who doubt in a literal Resurrection. Create an atmosphere where honest doubts can surface and be discussed, not shut down with a dismissive comment or glance.

Read Luke 24:36-53, or ask a volunteer to read today's passage aloud. Encourage everyone else to follow along in their own Bibles or in their participant guides.

God's Word: Luke 24:36-53

^{36} While they were still talking about this, Jesus himself stood among them and said to them, "Peace be with you."

^{37} They were startled and frightened, thinking they saw a ghost. ^{38} He said to them, "Why are you troubled, and why do doubts rise in your minds? ^{39} Look at my hands and my feet. It is I myself! Touch me and see; a ghost does not have flesh and bones, as you see I have."

^{40} When he had said this, he showed them his hands and feet. ^{41} And while they still did not believe it because of joy and amazement, he asked them, "Do you have anything here to eat?" ^{42} They gave him a piece of broiled fish, ^{43} and he took it and ate it in their presence.

^{44} He said to them, "This is what I told you while I was still with you: Everything must be fulfilled that is written about me in the Law of Moses, the Prophets and the Psalms."

^{45} Then he opened their minds so they could understand the Scriptures. ^{46} He told them, "This is what is written: The Messiah will suffer and rise from the dead on the third day, ^{47} and repentance for the forgiveness of sins will be preached in his name to all nations, beginning at Jerusalem. ^{48} You are witnesses of these things. ^{49} I am going to send you what my Father has promised; but stay in the city until you have been clothed with power from on high."

^{50} When he had led them out to the vicinity of Bethany, he lifted up his hands and blessed them. ^{51} While he was blessing them, he left them and was taken up into heaven. ^{52} Then they worshiped him and returned to Jerusalem with great joy. ^{53} And they stayed continually at the temple, praising God."

Let's take a moment to reflect on this passage.

- **What questions and thoughts come to mind when you read through this passage?**

Write down your initial thoughts and questions in your participant guide.

Give people a few minutes to jot down their questions or thoughts before moving forward. Have people do this on their own, not in groups. When everyone looks like they're ready, move to the next step.

GRAPPLING

A quick reminder: This is a safe place to share what we think and believe and what we doubt, as well. It's okay to ask hard questions and to not have all the answers. Jesus' followers were in exactly that spot after Jesus rose, and Jesus didn't condemn them. Rather, he met them where they were and gave them what they needed. Let's trust him to do the same with us.

Pray for people in the group to have the courage to ask the hard questions. Ask God to lead all of you as you seek the answers to those questions.

! LEADER LEARNING

By the end of this study, some who've taken part might be ready to make a deep heartfelt commitment to following Jesus—either for the first time or as a way to "renew their vows" with the Lord. Be ready to walk alongside any of the people in your group who want to take this step and to celebrate their decision with them.

BEHIND THE SCENES

The proofs of the physicality of Jesus' glorified body—that it had substance, could be touched, and could enjoy and consume food—turned out to be a big deal. During the early years of the church's existence, many false teachers crept in and tried to persuade the believers that Jesus was never a true human being—that he only appeared to be a man.

Nothing could be further from the truth.

Years after the Resurrection, when the apostles were combating these false ideas, they would have remembered how Jesus invited them to touch his hands and feet to reassure them he wasn't a ghost. He even sat down and ate with them. By doing this, Jesus demonstrated that his resurrection was real and that he was, indeed, alive.

With your small group, discuss the first question you'll find under the "Grappling" heading. You'll have about 5 minutes, and then I'll ask for groups to share what they talked about with the larger group.

LESSON 13: HOW CAN I KNOW JESUS IS REALLY ALIVE TODAY?

- **The disciples had ample evidence that Jesus had died...yet there he stood. In what ways did Jesus meet them where they were—emotionally, physically, spiritually, or in other ways?**

Allow about 5 minutes for discussion, and then have each group share something they feel is significant.

Let's talk about this next question as a large group. Jesus had been telling his followers for years that he would die and come back to life. But this was the first time they understood. Obviously it had something to do with him standing there! But Jesus also referred to Scriptures that had foretold these events.

- **Why do you think Jesus took the time to make this additional point even when he was standing right there in front of them? And does this have any implications for us all these years later?**

Allow time for different people to share their thoughts with the whole group. When several people have had a chance to respond, continue.

In our small groups, let's talk about our own insights and questions that we jotted down earlier.

Allow at least 10 minutes for groups to talk. Give a 1-minute "time to wrap it up!" alert so groups have time to finish their thoughts.

What's an idea or question that your group found interesting? Who'll share with the larger group something you brought up in your small group?

Allow a few minutes for groups to share. Depending on how much time you have left you can simply let groups report their insights and questions, or if you have time you can invite the larger group to respond to what was shared.

LEADER LEARNING

Some Christians can be very heady and logical about their faith, while others are more emotional and sensitive to the supernatural work of the Holy Spirit. Be sensitive to where each of your group members might be on this spectrum and work with them in ways that are meaningful to them. We can't insist fellow believers experience the Lord in the same ways we do. God works through the lives of people in many different ways—usually in ways that fit well with their personalities.

BEHIND THE SCENES

Did you know there are more than 350 prophecies about the Messiah in the Old Testament—and that Jesus fulfilled every single one of them to the smallest detail?

Jesus made it a point here—and with the disciples on the road to Emmaus—to show that everything predicted about him in the Law and through the Prophets came true. The odds of this happening with one person are astronomical—but not for the One of whom the prophecies spoke.

What do you think? Is Jesus really alive today? Jesus gave the disciples what they needed in order to know beyond a shadow of a doubt that what they were experiencing was real. How do you think the Lord fulfills this need for us today? What has been your experience in this area of affirming your faith?

I think it would be great to hear stories of how God has affirmed your faith and helped you know that Jesus is alive. Is anyone willing to share a story with the entire group?

Invite anyone who is willing to share about their own journey to faith or an event that led them to believe Jesus is truly alive. These stories from the lives of friends can be encouraging to those who are still grappling with issues of faith. If you're concerned that the lesson will go too long with this sharing, it's okay to say, "We need to wrap this up so we can finish on time, but I'd love to meet for coffee one evening this week to keep this conversation going!" and then make sure that happens. If people in your class are wanting to share what God is doing in their lives, make a way for that conversation to continue!

BEHIND THE SCENES

Luke tells us that Jesus "opened their minds" so they could understand the Scriptures. This is just a humble reminder that we would not be able to accurately comprehend a single word of the Bible if it were not for the work of the Holy Spirit in our hearts, enabling us to understand God's truth and how those truths apply to our lives.

GROWING

I hope this fearless conversation has encouraged you in your faith and helped you consider how you personally can know that Jesus is alive.

To wrap up this lesson, let's return to the overarching question that is posed by the title "Why Is Jesus

LESSON 13: HOW CAN I KNOW JESUS IS REALLY ALIVE TODAY? 117

Leader Guide

So Radical?" Every week as we've ended our lesson, we've had time to reflect on that question and add new thoughts based on what we'd studied that day. Now, after all these weeks of digging into the life of Jesus, how do you answer that question?

I'd like you to get back into your small groups and take about 3 minutes to look back through your notes from previous weeks. Share a few of the comments you wrote that still resonate with you today. Then see if your group can come up with one sentence that answers the question, Why is Jesus so radical? We'll share those back with the larger group.

Allow 5 to 8 minutes for groups to grapple with this question one last time. It will be a challenge to summarize in one sentence—but that's okay! When time is up, have each group share their sentence. Thank everyone for having such fearless conversations and really wrestling with the questions posed through this quarter of Sunday school. Then invite everyone into a time of open prayer.

Let's express our responses to God in a prayer. What does it mean to your own life that Jesus is radical? Perhaps it means that you are healed. Saved. Challenged. Filled with hope. Think of a simple way to express what it means to you personally.

I'm going to open us in prayer, and I'd like each person to pray as you are comfortable. Simply finish this sentence as a prayer: "Jesus, because you are so radical, I am ___."

Open the prayer with your own end to that sentence, and leave the time open for a moment so anyone else who wants to pray can. Then wrap up the prayer, thanking God for all that has been learned through this time and for the changes that have happened through the challenges of the conversations.

If you have the next quarter of curriculum with you, show everyone what's coming and let them know where to get their participant books.

Notes:

Notes: